MW01228574

No Grid Survival Projects

1000 Days of DIY Projects and Ideas for Self-Sufficiency and Resilience

M.T SMITH

Introduction

As society continues to evolve, many people are becoming increasingly interested in off-grid living. This type of lifestyle involves being completely self-sufficient and relying solely on renewable energy sources, local water sources, and homegrown food. The appeal of off-grid living stems from a desire to reduce dependence on the government, fossil fuels, and the modern conveniences that many people take for granted.

There are many reasons why off-grid living is becoming more popular. First and foremost, it provides a sense of independence and self-reliance. Many people are tired of being at the mercy of utility companies and rising energy costs, and they want to take control of their own energy usage. Off-grid living allows people to generate their own power and be completely self-sufficient in terms of their energy needs.

Secondly, off-grid living is a way to reduce one's impact on the environment. By living off the grid, people can minimize their carbon footprint and reduce their consumption of natural resources. This is a crucial consideration for those who are concerned about the state of the planet and want to do their part to preserve it.

Thirdly, off-grid living is an opportunity to reconnect with nature and live a simpler, more fulfilling life. Many people find that they are happier and more content when they are not constantly bombarded by the distractions of modern life. Living off the grid allows people to focus on what truly matters to them, whether that be spending time with family, pursuing hobbies, or simply enjoying the beauty of the natural world.

However, off-grid living is not for everyone. It requires a significant investment of time, money, and effort to set up and maintain an off-grid lifestyle. Furthermore, living off the grid can be challenging, especially for those who are used to the conveniences of modern life. It requires a willingness to learn new skills, adapt to changing circumstances, and be resourceful in the face of unexpected challenges.

That's why it's important to prepare yourself for a self-sufficient lifestyle before making the leap to off-grid living. This book is designed to help you do just that. We will provide you with the information and tools you need to make an informed decision about whether off-grid living is right for you, and to help you succeed if you decide to take the plunge.

In the following chapters, we will cover a wide range of topics related to off-grid living, including energy projects, water projects, food production, waste management, and much more. Our goal is to give you a comprehensive overview of what it takes to live off the grid and provide you with the practical knowledge and skills you need to make it a reality.

So if you're ready to embrace a simpler, more sustainable way of life, let's get started!

Chapter 1: Energy Projects

Energy is an essential aspect of modern life. Most people depend on the power grid for their daily energy needs. However, in the event of a disaster, power outages can occur, making it difficult to perform essential tasks such as cooking, heating, and lighting. Living off-grid means that you are not dependent on the power grid for your energy needs. Instead, you produce your own energy using alternative energy sources such as solar panels, wind turbines, and hydroelectric generators.

In recent years, there has been a growing interest in off-grid living. People are realizing the benefits of producing their own energy and reducing their dependence on fossil fuels. By producing their own energy, they can save money on energy bills, become more self-sufficient, and reduce their carbon footprint. This growing interest in off-grid living has led to an increase in the development of alternative energy solutions, making it easier than ever to produce your own energy.

In this section of the book, we will explore various energy projects that you can undertake to become more self-sufficient. We will cover DIY solar panel installation, building wind turbines, hydroelectric generators for off-grid energy, energy storage solutions for the homestead, biogas production for cooking and heating, using propane generators, and energy harvesting hand crank generators. With the information in this section, you will be equipped to produce your own energy and become more self-reliant.

1.1 DIY Solar Panel Installation

One of the most popular and effective ways to produce off-grid energy is through solar panels. Solar panels are devices that convert sunlight into electricity, providing a clean and renewable source of energy. Installing solar panels on your homestead can significantly reduce your energy bills and carbon footprint, and increase your self-sufficiency.

DIY solar panel installation is a great way to reduce the cost of solar panel installation while still reaping the benefits of solar energy. With some basic knowledge of electrical wiring and construction, it's possible to install your own solar panels and start producing your own energy.

Before starting your DIY solar panel installation project, it's essential to conduct a site analysis to determine the best location for your solar panels. The ideal location for solar panels is a south-facing roof that receives direct sunlight throughout the day. However, if a south-facing roof is not available, solar panels can also be installed on the ground or on a west or east-facing roof.

Once you have determined the best location for your solar panels, the next step is to design your solar panel system. This involves calculating the amount of electricity you need to produce and determining the number of solar panels required to meet that demand.

The next step is to install the solar panels on your roof or ground. This involves mounting the solar panels on a sturdy frame and connecting them to an inverter. The inverter is responsible for converting the DC electricity produced by the solar panels into AC electricity that can be used in your home.

Once the solar panels are installed, it's essential to conduct a safety inspection and test the system to ensure that it's functioning correctly. With proper installation and maintenance, a DIY solar panel system can provide clean and renewable energy for years to come.

In summary, DIY solar panel installation is an excellent way to produce off-grid energy and become more self-sufficient. By conducting a site analysis, designing your solar panel system, and properly installing and maintaining your solar panels, you can reduce your energy bills, increase your self-sufficiency, and reduce your carbon footprint.

1.2 Building Wind Turbines

Wind turbines are another popular and effective way to produce off-grid energy. Wind turbines harness the power of wind to generate electricity, providing a clean and renewable source of energy. Building your own wind turbine is a great way to reduce the cost of wind energy production while still reaping the benefits of wind power.

Before starting your DIY wind turbine project, it's essential to conduct a site analysis to determine the best location for your wind turbine. The ideal location for a wind turbine is an area with a consistent and strong wind flow, free from obstacles that could block the wind.

Once you have determined the best location for your wind turbine, the next step is to design your wind turbine system. This involves selecting the right components and determining the number of blades, tower height, and generator size required to meet your energy needs.

The next step is to construct the tower for your wind turbine. This involves selecting the appropriate materials, such as steel or wood, and building a sturdy tower that can withstand strong winds.

After the tower is constructed, the next step is to install the turbine itself. This involves installing the blades, rotor, and generator on top of the tower, connecting the components with appropriate wiring, and ensuring that everything is secure and properly aligned.

Once the wind turbine is installed, it's essential to conduct a safety inspection and test the system to ensure that it's functioning correctly. With proper installation and maintenance, a DIY wind turbine can provide clean and renewable energy for years to come.

In summary, building your own wind turbine is an excellent way to produce off-grid energy and become more self-sufficient. By conducting a site analysis, designing your wind turbine system, and properly constructing and installing your wind turbine, you can reduce your energy bills, increase your self-sufficiency, and reduce your carbon footprint.

There are a variety of different designs and types of wind turbines that can be built depending on the resources available, budget, and energy requirements. Some of the most common types of wind turbines include horizontal-axis wind turbines (HAWT) and vertical-axis wind turbines (VAWT).

Horizontal-axis wind turbines are the most commonly used type of wind turbine and typically consist of two or three blades mounted on a horizontal axis. They are efficient at converting wind energy into electricity and can be built to various sizes to meet the energy requirements of different households.

Vertical-axis wind turbines, on the other hand, have their blades mounted on a vertical axis, making them more suitable for locations with unpredictable or turbulent wind patterns. They can also be built to a smaller scale than

HAWTs, making them a great option for households with limited space or budget.

When building your own wind turbine, it's important to consider the overall cost of the project. While building your own wind turbine can be cheaper than purchasing a pre-built system, there are still significant costs involved, such as the cost of materials, tower construction, and installation. However, over time, the savings in energy costs can offset these initial costs, making it a worthwhile investment for those looking to live off-grid.

Overall, building your own wind turbine is a great way to produce clean and renewable energy and become more self-sufficient. By choosing the right design, constructing a sturdy tower, and ensuring proper installation and maintenance, you can enjoy the benefits of off-grid energy for years to come.

1.3 Hydroelectric Generators for Off-Grid Energy

Hydroelectric generators are an excellent source of off-grid energy and are particularly effective in locations with a steady supply of running water, such as a stream or river. They work by using the force of water to spin a turbine, which in turn powers a generator to produce electricity.

Building a hydroelectric generator requires a bit more planning and construction than some other off-grid energy sources, but it can provide a reliable and consistent source of power. To build a hydroelectric generator, you will need to identify a suitable water source, such as a stream or river with a consistent flow rate, and determine the amount of power you need to generate.

One common type of hydroelectric generator is the micro-hydro generator, which is ideal for off-grid homes or small communities. A micro-hydro generator typically produces between 1000 and 5000 watts of power and can be built with a variety of materials and designs depending on the water source and energy requirements.

When building a hydroelectric generator, it's important to consider the environmental impact on the surrounding area. It's crucial to ensure that the installation of the generator doesn't negatively impact the ecosystem and wildlife in the area. You may need to obtain permits and permissions from local authorities before starting the construction.

There are several factors to consider when building a hydroelectric generator for off-grid energy. One of the primary considerations is the head, or the vertical distance between the water source and the generator. The higher the head, the greater the potential energy production, but higher heads also require more expensive equipment and more complex installation.

Another important factor to consider is the flow rate of the water source. The greater the flow rate, the more energy the generator can produce. However, if the flow rate is too low, the generator may not be able to produce enough energy to meet the needs of the household or community.

There are two primary types of hydroelectric generators: impulse and reaction turbines. Impulse turbines are generally used for high head applications, while reaction turbines are better suited for low head applications. The choice of turbine will depend on the specific water source and energy requirements.

In addition to the turbine, a hydroelectric generator system will also require a penstock, which is a pipe that transports the water from the source to the turbine. The penstock must be properly sized to ensure a consistent flow of water to the turbine and must be designed to handle the pressure of the water.

Another consideration when building a hydroelectric generator is the environmental impact. While hydroelectric generators are generally considered a clean source of energy, the construction and operation of the generator can have an impact on the surrounding ecosystem. It's important to carefully consider the potential impacts and take steps to minimize them.

Maintenance is also an important factor to consider when building a hydroelectric generator. Regular inspections and upkeep are necessary to ensure the generator is functioning properly and to prevent damage or accidents. It's important to have a maintenance plan in place and to regularly monitor the generator to ensure it continues to produce energy efficiently and safely.

In terms of cost, hydroelectric generators can be expensive to build and install, especially for higher head applications. However, once the generator is in place, the cost of energy production is relatively low and the generator can provide a reliable source of energy for many years.

Overall, building a hydroelectric generator can be a challenging but rewarding project for those looking to live off-grid. With careful planning and construction, a hydroelectric generator can provide a reliable and sustainable source of energy for years to come. It's important to work with experienced professionals and obtain the necessary permits and permissions to ensure a safe and environmentally friendly installation.

1.4 Energy Storage Solutions for the Homestead

When generating your own energy off the grid, it's important to have a way to store excess energy for use when energy production is low or during periods of high demand. Energy storage solutions for the homestead can come in various forms, including batteries, pumped hydro storage, and compressed air energy storage.

Batteries are one of the most commonly used energy storage solutions for off-grid systems. They store excess energy generated during times of high production for use during periods of low production. Batteries come in various types, including lead-acid, lithium-ion, and nickel-cadmium. Each type has its own advantages and disadvantages, and it's important to choose the right type of battery for your specific energy needs.

Pumped hydro storage is another energy storage solution that works by using excess energy to pump water to a higher elevation, where it can be stored as potential energy. When energy is needed, the water is released, and the potential energy is converted to kinetic energy, which can be used to generate electricity. This method of energy storage is more commonly used in larger-scale applications but can be adapted for use in smaller off-grid systems.

Compressed air energy storage works by compressing air during periods of high energy production and storing it in a tank. When energy is needed, the compressed air is released, which drives a turbine to generate electricity. This method of energy storage is relatively new and still in the research and development phase, but it has the potential to be a low-cost and efficient solution for off-grid energy storage.

When choosing an energy storage solution for your homestead, it's important to consider factors such as cost, efficiency, reliability, and maintenance requirements. Each solution has its own advantages and disadvantages, and it's important to choose the one that best meets your specific energy needs and budget.

Another energy storage option to consider is flywheel energy storage. This method uses the kinetic energy of a spinning rotor to store energy. When energy is needed, the rotor slows down, and the kinetic energy is converted into electrical energy.

It's important to note that energy storage solutions can be expensive, so it's important to carefully consider your energy needs and usage patterns before investing in a particular solution. It's also a good idea to consult with an energy expert or professional to ensure that you choose the most efficient and cost-effective option for your off-grid energy needs.

In addition to energy storage solutions, it's important to also consider ways to optimize energy usage on your homestead. This can include using energy-efficient appliances, reducing energy waste, and implementing energy-saving practices such as turning off lights and electronics when not in use.

Overall, energy storage solutions are a key component of any off-grid energy system, allowing for reliable energy production and use even during periods of fluctuating energy production. Proper planning and consideration of energy storage solutions can help ensure a self-sufficient and sustainable homestead.

1.5 Biogas Production for Cooking and Heating

Biogas production is a sustainable and cost-effective way to produce fuel for cooking and heating on an off-grid homestead. Biogas is a renewable energy source that is generated through the anaerobic digestion of organic waste such as food scraps, animal manure, and crop residues. This process produces methane gas, which can be captured and used as a fuel for cooking, heating, and electricity generation.

To set up a biogas production system, you'll need a biogas digester, which is a container designed to facilitate the anaerobic digestion process. There are many different designs and types of biogas digesters, ranging from simple homemade designs to more complex commercial systems. The basic principle behind all biogas digesters is the same: organic waste is added to the digester, where it is broken down by bacteria in the absence of oxygen, producing biogas as a byproduct.

One common type of biogas digester is the "floating drum" design. This consists of a large, airtight drum that floats on top of a pit or tank containing the organic waste. As the waste is digested, biogas is produced and captured in the drum, where it can be piped to a stove or other appliance for use.

Another type of biogas digester is the "fixed dome" design. This consists of a concrete or brick dome-shaped structure that is buried in the ground, with a gas outlet pipe and an inlet for adding organic waste. As the waste is digested, biogas is produced and stored in the dome, where it can be piped to a stove or other appliance.

Biogas production has many benefits for off-grid living, including:

- **Cost-effective fuel source:** Biogas production can provide a sustainable source of fuel for cooking and heating that is much cheaper than traditional fossil fuels.

- **Reduces waste:** By using organic waste as a feedstock for biogas production, you can reduce waste and create a valuable resource.
- **Low emissions:** Biogas is a clean-burning fuel that produces low levels of emissions and pollutants, making it a sustainable and environmentally friendly option.
- **Increases self-sufficiency:** By producing your own fuel on your homestead, you can become more self-sufficient and reduce your reliance on traditional energy sources.

In addition to being a sustainable source of energy, biogas production also helps to manage waste. Biogas can be produced from a variety of organic materials, including kitchen waste, manure, and plant residues. The production process involves collecting and storing the organic material in an airtight container, where it is broken down by bacteria in the absence of oxygen. This process is known as anaerobic digestion and produces biogas, which is primarily composed of methane, carbon dioxide, and small amounts of other gasses.

The biogas can be used for cooking, heating, or generating electricity. It is important to note that biogas production requires careful monitoring and management to ensure that the process runs smoothly and the biogas is of high quality. The biogas can be stored in a tank and used as needed.

There are several benefits to using biogas for cooking and heating. First, it is a renewable energy source that reduces reliance on fossil fuels. Second, it helps to manage waste and reduce greenhouse gas emissions from organic waste that would otherwise decompose in landfills. Third, biogas production can also produce nutrient-rich fertilizer as a byproduct, which can be used to improve soil quality and support plant growth.

To set up a biogas system, you will need an airtight container or digester, as well as a source of organic material to feed into the digester. The digester can be made from a variety of materials, including concrete, plastic, or metal. The organic material should be fed into the digester regularly to maintain the anaerobic conditions necessary for biogas production. The biogas produced can be stored and used as needed.

There are different types of biogas systems available, ranging from simple homemade designs to more complex commercial systems. Some of the factors to consider when setting up a biogas system include the size of the system, the type of organic material to be used, and the desired end use of the biogas.

One common type of biogas system is a fixed dome digester. This type of digester is made from a concrete or brick structure with an airtight dome that allows for gas storage. The organic material is fed into the digester through an inlet pipe, and the biogas is collected and stored in the dome. A gas outlet pipe is used to connect the digester to the gas appliances.

Another type of biogas system is a floating drum digester. This type of digester uses a flexible dome or bag that floats on top of the organic material. The biogas is collected and stored in a separate container, and the gas is fed to the appliances using a gas outlet pipe.

When setting up a biogas system, it is important to ensure that the system is properly sized and designed to meet the energy needs of the household. The type of organic material used can also impact the biogas production and quality, so it is important to select materials that are easily digestible and have a high methane content.

To produce biogas, organic material is fed into the digester and allowed to break down in the absence of oxygen. This process, called anaerobic digestion, produces a mixture of gasses, including methane, carbon dioxide, and trace amounts of other gasses.

The methane in biogas is the key component that makes it a useful source of energy. Methane has a high energy content and can be used for cooking, heating, and electricity generation. In addition to the energy benefits, biogas production also has environmental benefits, as it helps to reduce greenhouse gas emissions from organic waste and promotes the use of renewable energy.

When setting up a biogas system, it is important to consider the feedstock that will be used to produce the biogas. Common feedstocks include animal manure, food waste, and agricultural residues. The choice of feedstock will depend on local availability and the energy needs of the household.

In addition to producing biogas, the anaerobic digestion process also produces a nutrient-rich fertilizer that can be used to improve soil fertility and crop yields. This provides a valuable source of organic fertilizer for off-grid farming and gardening.

Overall, biogas production is a valuable and sustainable energy source for off-grid living. It helps to manage waste, reduces reliance on fossil fuels, and provides a source of renewable energy for cooking, heating, and electricity generation. With careful planning and management, biogas systems can be an effective way to achieve self-sufficiency and resilience in off-grid living.

1.6 Using Propane Generators

Propane generators are an excellent option for off-grid living as they provide a reliable and efficient source of electricity. Propane is a clean-burning fuel, which means it produces less emissions and is less harmful to the environment compared to gasoline or diesel generators.

To use a propane generator, you will need to purchase a generator that is specifically designed to run on propane. These generators are readily available at most hardware or home improvement stores. Once you have your generator, you will need to connect it to a propane tank. Propane tanks can be purchased or rented from local propane suppliers.

When using a propane generator, it's important to follow proper safety precautions. Always read the manufacturer's instructions carefully and make sure to operate the generator in a well-ventilated area. Never use a propane generator indoors or in an enclosed space, as this can be extremely dangerous.

Propane generators also require regular maintenance to ensure they operate properly. This includes changing the oil, air filter, and spark plug on a regular basis. It's also important to store propane tanks properly and to check them for leaks before use.

Propane generators have several advantages over other types of generators. Propane is readily available and can be stored for long periods of time without degrading, making it an excellent fuel source for emergency situations. Propane generators are also quieter than gasoline or diesel generators, which can be a major advantage for those living in close proximity to neighbors.

However, there are also some disadvantages to using propane generators. Propane is less efficient than gasoline, which means that you will need to use more fuel to generate the same amount of electricity. Propane generators can also be more expensive to purchase initially than other types of generators.

When choosing a propane generator, it is important to consider your specific energy needs. Propane generators come in a range of sizes, with different wattage capacities. The larger the generator, the more power it can produce, but also the more expensive it will be.

Another important factor to consider is the generator's runtime. This is the amount of time the generator can operate continuously on a single tank of propane. The longer the runtime, the less frequently you will need to refill the propane tank, which can be particularly important during emergencies when it may be difficult to obtain propane.

When installing a propane generator, it is important to follow all safety precautions. Propane is a flammable gas, and improper installation or use of a propane generator can be dangerous or even deadly. Make sure to install the generator in a well-ventilated area and keep the propane tank away from sources of heat or flame.

Propane generators are also a popular choice for backup power during emergencies, such as power outages caused by severe weather or natural disasters. Because propane can be stored for long periods of time without going bad, it can provide a reliable source of energy when other sources may not be available.

In addition to powering your home, propane generators can also be used to power tools and equipment on your homestead. This can be particularly useful for those who engage in homesteading activities, such as farming or woodworking, that require the use of power tools.

When using a propane generator, it is important to maintain it properly to ensure it continues to function effectively. This may include regularly changing the oil, cleaning the air filter, and checking the spark plug. You should also store your propane tank in a safe and secure location, away from potential sources of ignition.

Overall, propane generators can be an excellent option for off-grid living, particularly for those who live in areas with limited access to other sources of renewable energy. By choosing the right size and type of generator and taking all necessary safety precautions, you can create a reliable and sustainable off-grid power system that meets all of your electricity needs.

1.7 Energy Harvesting Hand Crank Generators

Hand crank generators are a great way to produce energy off-grid without relying on traditional power sources. They can be used to power small devices, recharge batteries, and provide emergency backup power. Hand crank generators can be used in various situations, such as camping, hiking, or during power outages.

There are many types of hand crank generators available on the market, but they all work on the same principle of converting mechanical energy into electrical energy. They consist of a hand crank attached to a dynamo or generator, which produces electricity when the crank is turned.

When selecting a hand crank generator, consider the amount of energy you need to produce and the devices you intend to power. Some hand crank generators can produce more power than others, and some come with built-in batteries or USB ports for charging devices.

To get the most out of your hand crank generator, it is important to use it efficiently. This means turning the crank at a steady pace, not overloading the generator, and using energy-efficient devices. It is also important to maintain the generator by keeping it clean and dry, and replacing any worn parts.

Hand crank generators are a versatile and reliable source of off-grid energy that can be used in various situations. By incorporating them into your off-grid energy system, you can increase your self-sufficiency and resilience in the face of power outages or other emergencies.

One benefit of using hand crank generators is that they don't require any external energy sources, such as wind or sun, making them useful in situations where other energy sources may not be available. They are also relatively easy to construct, making them a good option for a DIY project.

To build a hand crank generator, you will need a few basic components: a DC motor, a flywheel, a crank arm, and a housing to hold everything in place. The DC motor is the heart of the generator, and it will convert the mechanical energy from the crank arm into electrical energy. The flywheel helps to store energy, allowing the generator to produce a consistent output even when the crank is not being turned at a constant speed.

Once you have built your hand crank generator, you can use it to power a variety of devices, such as lights, radios, or small appliances. However, it is important to note that hand crank generators produce a relatively small amount of power compared to other energy sources, so they may not be sufficient for powering larger devices or appliances.

Overall, hand crank generators can be a useful addition to an off-grid energy system, providing a reliable source of electricity in situations where other sources may not be available. With a bit of DIY know-how, it is possible to build a simple and effective hand crank generator that can help you become more self-sufficient and resilient in the face of unexpected challenges.

Chapter 2: Water Projects

Water is a crucial element of survival, and finding a clean and reliable source of water is essential for living off-grid. While there are many water sources available in nature, such as rivers, lakes, and streams, these sources may not always be safe to drink from. Moreover, the water table may be too deep to access, or the location may not receive sufficient rainfall to sustain a homestead.

This is where water projects come in, which can help homesteaders collect, store, and filter water in a sustainable and cost-effective manner. In this section of the book, we will explore a variety of water projects that can be used to ensure a reliable source of clean water for drinking, cooking, and cleaning. We will cover water collection methods, well drilling, rainwater harvesting, and water treatment systems that can be built from simple materials.

The water projects in this section are designed to help homesteaders become self-sufficient when it comes to their water supply, regardless of where they live. Whether you are in a dry climate or an area with abundant rainfall, there are water projects that can be adapted to your specific needs and location. By implementing these water projects, you can ensure that you always have access to clean and safe water, no matter what challenges you may face off-grid.

2.1 Collecting and Storing Rainwater

Collecting and storing rainwater is an essential part of off-grid living, especially if you live in an area with limited access to clean water sources. Fortunately, collecting rainwater is a simple and cost-effective way to ensure you have access to clean water for your daily needs.

To collect rainwater, you'll need a system that includes a catchment surface, gutters, downspouts, and a storage tank. The catchment surface can be your roof or any other surface that is clean and sloped to allow water to flow into the gutters. The gutters should be properly sized to handle the amount of rainfall in your area and should be cleaned regularly to prevent blockages.

The downspouts are used to channel the water from the gutters into the storage tank. You can use PVC pipes or other materials that are durable and resistant to corrosion. The storage tank should be made of a food-grade material such as plastic or stainless steel, and it should be equipped with a cover to prevent debris and insects from getting inside.

It's important to filter the rainwater before using it for drinking, cooking, or bathing. You can use a combination of filters to remove sediment, debris, and microorganisms. A basic filtration system may include a pre-filter to remove large particles, a sediment filter to remove smaller particles, and a carbon filter to remove chemicals and odors.

In addition to collecting rainwater, it's also important to conserve water and use it wisely. This can be done by using low-flow faucets, showerheads, and toilets, fixing leaks promptly, and using graywater for non-potable uses such as watering plants and flushing toilets.

To ensure that the rainwater collected is safe to use, it is important to filter it before storage. This can be done using a basic filter made from a 5-gallon bucket. Simply drill a hole near the bottom of the bucket and attach a spigot. Inside the bucket, place a layer of sand, followed by a layer of gravel, and then a layer of activated charcoal. The sand and gravel will remove larger particles and debris, while the activated charcoal will remove any impurities and improve the taste of the water.

When it comes to storing rainwater, there are several options available. One of the simplest and most affordable is to use a collection barrel. These can be purchased at most hardware stores and are typically made from food-grade plastic. They come in a range of sizes, but a 55-gallon barrel is a good starting point for most households.

In addition to collection barrels, there are also more advanced rainwater harvesting systems available. These can include pumps and filtration systems to provide a more reliable source of clean water for the home. However, these systems can be more expensive and complex to install, so it is important to do your research before investing in one.

To maximize the efficiency of a rainwater collection system, it is important to ensure that the water is properly stored. The simplest method of storage is to use large, food-grade plastic drums or tanks, which can hold hundreds or even thousands of gallons of water. These tanks should be placed on a level, stable surface and securely fastened to prevent them from tipping over.

It is also important to prevent contamination of the water. The collection system should be designed to prevent debris, such as leaves and twigs, from entering the tank. Additionally, it is recommended to install a filter to remove any remaining sediment, which can accumulate over time and affect the water quality.

To maintain the quality of the stored water, it is recommended to periodically clean the tank and disinfect the water. This can be done by draining the tank and scrubbing the interior with a non-toxic cleaner, followed by a thorough rinse. Chlorine can also be used to disinfect the water, but it is important to follow the manufacturer's instructions carefully to avoid over-chlorination.

In addition to storing rainwater, it is also important to have a backup water supply in case of emergencies. This can include a well, a spring, or even a nearby stream or lake. However, it is important to ensure that the water source is safe for consumption and to have a proper filtration system in place.

Overall, collecting and storing rainwater is a simple and effective way to ensure a reliable source of water for your off-grid homestead. By following these guidelines, you can maximize the efficiency of your collection system and ensure the safety and quality of your stored water.

2.2 Building a Water Well

Building a water well is a reliable and self-sustaining method of obtaining water for off-grid living. While drilling a well may seem like a daunting task, it is possible to do it yourself with the right tools and techniques. Here are the basic steps to follow:

- **Location**: When choosing a location for your well, it's important to consider a few key factors. First, you'll need to locate a spot that has a good water source underground. This can typically be determined by consulting with a professional well driller or hydrologist, who can assess the geology of the area and identify potential water sources.

In addition to the water source, you'll want to consider the accessibility of the location. Make sure that the location is easily accessible to your well drilling equipment and that there are no obstacles that may hinder the drilling process.

Another important factor to consider is the distance of your well from potential sources of contamination. Ensure that your well is located far enough away from septic systems, livestock areas, and other potential sources of pollution to prevent contamination of your drinking water.

Lastly, you may also need to obtain permits and follow local regulations when drilling a well. Be sure to research the regulations in your area and obtain any necessary permits before beginning construction.

- **Equipment:** You will need to gather the necessary equipment, including a drilling rig or water well kit, drill bits, casing pipe, gravel, and a well screen. You may also need a hand pump or electric pump depending on your needs.

- **Drilling:** Once you have located the ideal spot for your well and obtained the necessary equipment, you can begin drilling. The type of drilling method used will depend on the geology of the area and the depth of the well required.

One common drilling method is cable tool drilling, which involves repeatedly lifting and dropping a heavy bit on a cable to break up the rock and soil. Another method is rotary drilling, which uses a drill bit that rotates to break up the rock and soil. Both methods can be done by hand or with a drilling rig.

As you drill, it's important to keep the hole clean and free of debris. This can be done by using a bailer, which is a device that can remove debris and water from the hole. You may also need to use a casing, which is a pipe that is installed into the well to prevent the sides from collapsing and to protect the water quality.

Once the well is drilled to the desired depth, a pump can be installed to bring water to the surface. It's important to test the water quality to ensure it is safe to drink before using it for any purpose.

Building a water well can be a complex and time-consuming process, but it can provide a reliable source of water for your off-grid lifestyle. If you're not comfortable doing it yourself, it's important to hire a professional well driller to ensure the job is done correctly and safely.

Casing: Once the well has been drilled to the desired depth, the next step is to install the casing. The casing is a long, hollow pipe that is inserted into the hole to prevent it from collapsing and to keep out contaminants.

The size and material of the casing depend on the size and depth of the well, as well as the geology of the area. In general, casings are made of materials such as PVC, steel, or concrete.

The casing is inserted into the well and lowered down to the bottom using a casing hammer or other equipment. The casing should extend above the ground level to prevent surface water from entering the well.

The space between the casing and the drilled hole is filled with gravel or other material to provide stability and prevent the casing from shifting. This also allows water to flow into the well while keeping out sand and other debris.

After the casing is installed, a well cap or seal is attached to the top of the casing to prevent contamination from entering the well. The well cap should be airtight and watertight to keep out insects, rodents, and other animals.

Overall, casing is an essential part of the water well drilling process that helps ensure clean, safe, and reliable water for your homestead.

Well screen: Once the well has been drilled and the casing has been inserted, it is important to install a well screen. A well screen is a perforated pipe that allows water to enter the well while preventing sand and other debris from entering. Without a well screen, the water in the well could become contaminated, reducing its quality and making it unsafe to drink.

To install a well screen, follow these steps:

1. Measure the length of the casing and cut the well screen to the same length.
2. Slide the well screen down into the casing. Be sure that the bottom of the well screen is at least 2 feet above the bottom of the well.
3. Attach a threaded cap to the bottom of the well screen.
4. Attach a connector to the top of the well screen.
5. Lower the pump and piping into the well.
6. Connect the pump and piping to the connector on the top of the well screen.
7. Fill the well with water to test the pump and ensure that it is functioning properly.
8. Installing a well screen is a critical step in the construction of a water well. Be sure to follow

all safety procedures and use appropriate equipment to avoid injury.

Pump: After the well screen is installed, the next step is to install a pump. The pump is what will draw water up from the well and deliver it to your home or storage tank. There are several types of pumps that can be used for this purpose, including submersible pumps and jet pumps.

Submersible pumps are installed directly inside the well and are designed to push water up to the surface. They are typically more expensive than jet pumps but are more efficient and require less maintenance.

Jet pumps, on the other hand, are installed above the ground and use suction to pull water up from the well. They are less expensive than submersible pumps but are less efficient and require more maintenance.

Once the pump is installed, it needs to be connected to your home's plumbing system or storage tank. This can be done using a variety of different piping materials, such as PVC or copper.

It's important to note that the size and type of pump you need will depend on several factors, such as the depth of your well, the amount of water you need to pump, and the pressure requirements of your plumbing system. It's best to consult with a professional well driller or pump installer to ensure that you choose the right pump for your needs.

Building a water well is a significant investment in time and money, but it provides a reliable source of water for off-grid living. With proper maintenance, a well can last for many years and provide water for generations to come.

2.3 Finding and Using Outside Water Source

When living off the grid, it's essential to find alternative sources of water beyond what you can collect and store on your property. There are several ways to find outside water sources, including:

Rivers and streams: If you live near a river or stream, you can collect water for domestic and irrigation purposes. However, it's essential to ensure that the water is clean and safe to drink. You can use a water filter, UV purification systems, or boiling to make the water safe.

Lakes and ponds: Lakes and ponds are also a good source of water. However, you need to be careful because the water can be contaminated with algae or other pollutants. You should test the water to ensure that it's safe to drink, and you can also use a filter or boil the water to make it safe.

Springs: Springs are a natural source of water and are usually clean and safe to drink. If you're lucky enough to have a spring on your property, you can use it as your primary water source.

Wells: You can also dig a well to find water. However, this can be an expensive and time-consuming process, and you'll need to check with your local authorities to see if you need any permits.

Once you've found an outside water source, you'll need to collect and transport the water to your property. You can use buckets, jugs, or a water pump to collect the water and transport it to your property. You can also use gravity-fed irrigation systems to water your plants and crops.

It's essential to ensure that the water you collect and use is safe to drink. You can test the water regularly to check for any contaminants, and you can also use filtration systems or boil the water to make it safe. With proper planning and preparation, you can find and use outside water sources to supplement your off-grid water supply.

2.4 Greywater Treatment Systems

Greywater is wastewater that comes from sources such as showers, sinks, and washing machines. It can be collected and treated to be reused for non-potable purposes such as irrigation, flushing toilets, and washing clothes. In an off-grid living situation, greywater treatment systems can be a great way to conserve water and reduce the demand on freshwater sources. Here are some ways to implement greywater treatment systems for your homestead:

Simple filtration system: A simple greywater treatment system can be set up using a series of filters to remove large debris and particles from the greywater. This can be done by using a gravel or sand filter, followed by a finer mesh filter. The filtered water can then be used for irrigation or flushing toilets.

Here are some additional details on this approach:

A simple filtration system for greywater treatment typically involves passing the water through a series of filters to remove contaminants. The filters may be made of sand, gravel, or other materials that can trap particles and bacteria. The system may also include a settling tank, which allows larger particles to settle to the bottom before the water is filtered.

To set up a simple filtration system, you will need to:

• Determine the flow rate of your greywater. This will help you determine how much filtering capacity you need.

• Choose a filtration medium. Sand and gravel are commonly used, but you can also use other materials such as crushed stone or coconut coir.

• Construct a settling tank. This can be made of concrete, plastic, or other materials.

- Set up your filtration system. The filters can be arranged in a series of layers, with the coarsest filter material at the top and the finest at the bottom.

- Add a pump if necessary. If your greywater is not flowing under gravity, you will need to add a pump to move it through the system.

- Monitor and maintain the system. Regular maintenance is important to ensure that the filters are working properly and to prevent clogs.

Overall, a simple filtration system can be an effective and affordable way to treat greywater for reuse. However, it may not be suitable for all situations, such as where there is high organic content or other contaminants in the water. In these cases, more advanced treatment systems may be required.

Constructed wetland: A constructed wetland is another type of greywater treatment system that can be used in off-grid living situations. This system works by mimicking the natural processes of a wetland, which naturally filters and purifies water.

To build a constructed wetland, you will need a large area of land that is not being used for any other purpose. The size of the wetland will depend on the amount of greywater that needs to be treated. Ideally, the wetland should be located downstream from any drinking water sources, to prevent contamination.

The first step in building a constructed wetland is to excavate the area to create a basin that is about 2 to 3 feet deep. The bottom of the basin should be lined with a layer of gravel or rocks to help with drainage. Next, a layer of sand and a layer of soil are added on top of the gravel layer.

Once the layers are in place, wetland plants are added to the basin. These plants are specifically chosen for their ability to absorb nutrients and filter water. Common wetland plants include cattails, bulrushes, and water irises.

As greywater enters the wetland, the plants and microorganisms work together to break down and remove contaminants. The gravel and sand layers help filter the water as it flows through the wetland. Once the water has been treated, it can be used for irrigation or discharged into a nearby stream or pond.

A constructed wetland is a low-maintenance and cost-effective way to treat greywater in an off-grid living situation. However, it does require a significant amount of space and may not be feasible for all properties. Additionally, it is important to properly maintain the wetland to ensure it continues to function effectively.

Membrane filtration: Membrane filtration is a process of separating particles and impurities from water by passing it through a semipermeable membrane. This method is highly effective at removing pollutants, bacteria, and viruses, making it ideal for purifying water for drinking or irrigation purposes.

There are different types of membrane filtration systems, including reverse osmosis (RO), nanofiltration (NF), and ultrafiltration (UF). RO is the most commonly used method in off-grid water projects due to its high efficiency and ability to remove a wide range of contaminants.

In an RO system, water is pushed through a semipermeable membrane under high pressure, which separates the contaminants from the water. The purified water then goes through a post-treatment process to adjust pH levels and add minerals.

One disadvantage of membrane filtration is that it requires a significant amount of energy to operate, as the high pressure needed to push water through the membrane requires a powerful pump. Therefore, it may not be suitable for all off-grid living situations, especially those with limited access to energy.

Overall, membrane filtration is an effective water treatment option for off-grid living, but careful consideration of energy usage and maintenance requirements should be taken before choosing this method.

.

It is important to note that greywater treatment systems require regular maintenance and monitoring to ensure that the water is safe for reuse. Additionally, it is important to check local regulations and obtain necessary permits before installing a greywater treatment system.

2.5 DIY Water Filtration Methods

DIY water filtration methods can be a cost-effective and sustainable solution for off-grid living. Here are some popular methods:

1. **Gravity-fed drip filter:** A gravity-fed drip filter uses a container, such as a 5-gallon bucket, with holes drilled in the bottom. Layers of gravel, sand, and activated charcoal are placed inside the bucket, and the contaminated water is poured into the top. As the water passes through the layers, impurities are removed, and clean water drips out of the bottom into a collection container.

2. **Ceramic filter:** A ceramic filter is a simple but effective filtration method. It works by using a porous ceramic material that filters out impurities as the water passes through it. The ceramic filter is often combined with activated charcoal for even more effective filtration.

3. **Solar still:** A solar still uses the heat of the sun to evaporate contaminated water, which then condenses on a clear plastic cover and drips into a collection container. This method can be useful in arid regions with high levels of sunlight.

4. **Reverse osmosis:** Reverse osmosis is a highly effective filtration method that uses a semi-permeable membrane to remove impurities. A reverse osmosis system can be purchased or built DIY with a high-pressure pump, a membrane filter, and activated charcoal.

5. **UV treatment:** UV treatment is a non-chemical method of water purification that uses ultraviolet light to kill bacteria and other harmful organisms. A UV lamp can be used in combination with other filtration methods for added effectiveness.

It's important to note that DIY water filtration methods may not be as effective as commercial systems, and regular maintenance is necessary to ensure proper function. Additionally, it's always recommended to test water quality periodically to ensure that it's safe for consumption.

2.6 Boiling Water for Safety

Boiling water is one of the simplest and most effective methods for ensuring safe drinking water. It kills most types of bacteria, viruses, and parasites that can cause illness. The process of boiling water is simple and can be done with minimal equipment.

To boil water, you will need a heat source, a pot, and clean water. The pot should be made of a material that can withstand high temperatures and be used for cooking, such as stainless steel, aluminum, or enamel-coated metal. The water should be free of debris and contaminants, such as dirt, leaves, or chemicals.

The basic steps for boiling water are as follows:

1. Fill a pot with clean water. If the water is cloudy, let it settle and clear before boiling.
2. Place the pot on a heat source, such as a stove or campfire.
3. Bring the water to a rolling boil.
4. Allow the water to boil for at least one minute.

5. Turn off the heat source and allow the water to cool.

After the water has boiled and cooled, it can be used for drinking, cooking, or other purposes. Boiling water is a reliable method for ensuring safe drinking water in emergency situations, such as during a natural disaster or camping trip.

It is important to note that boiling water may not remove all types of contaminants, such as chemicals or heavy metals. In these cases, additional treatment methods may be necessary. Additionally, boiling water does not make it taste better, so if the water has an unpleasant taste or odor, additional treatment methods may be needed.

2.7 Building a Solar Still for Water Purification

Building a solar still is an effective method of water purification that utilizes the sun's energy to evaporate water and then condense the resulting vapor into a clean container. The process can remove salt, minerals, and other impurities from water, making it safe for consumption.

To build a solar still, you will need a few simple materials, including a clear plastic sheet, a digging tool, a collection container, and a rock or other weight.

Here are the steps to building a solar still:

1. **Find a sunny spot with moist soil:** The location should have access to plenty of sunlight and be near a water source. The soil should be moist to ensure the maximum amount of water can be collected.
2. **Dig a hole:** Using your digging tool, dig a hole in the ground that is about 2-3 feet deep and wide enough to fit your collection container.
3. **Place the collection container in the hole:** Put your collection container in the center of the hole. Make sure it is stable and won't tip over.
4. **Surround the container with impure water:** Fill the hole with impure water until the water level is just below the lip of the container.
5. **Cover the hole with the clear plastic sheet:** Stretch the plastic sheet tightly over the hole, making sure there are no gaps or wrinkles. Place a rock or other weight on the center of the sheet, directly above the collection container.
6. **Wait for the sun to do its work:** As the sun shines on the plastic sheet, it will heat up the water in the hole, causing it to evaporate. The water vapor will then condense on the underside of the plastic sheet and drip down into the collection container.
7. **Collect the purified water:** Once enough water has collected in the container, remove it and enjoy!

It's important to note that this method may not be suitable for all water sources, and it's recommended to test the water for contaminants before using a solar still. Additionally, this method may not produce enough water for larger groups or extended periods of time.

2.8 Digging a Pond or Reservoir for Water Storage

Water is a vital resource, especially for those living off-grid. One way to ensure a steady supply of water is by digging a pond or reservoir for water storage. This can be done using basic tools, such as shovels and pickaxes, and with the help of some heavy machinery if available. In this section, we will discuss the steps involved in digging a pond or reservoir for water storage.

1. Planning
Before starting any digging, it is important to plan the size and location of the pond or reservoir. The location should be in an area that receives sufficient rainfall, and it should be accessible for easy maintenance. The size of the pond or reservoir will depend on the needs of the homestead, such as water usage and livestock   needs.

2. Marking
Once the location has been selected, the area should be marked using stakes or paint. The marking should reflect the shape and size of the pond or reservoir. It is important to remember that the pond or reservoir should have a depth

of at least 6 feet to prevent it from drying out during periods of low rainfall.

3. Excavation
Can be done using a variety of tools, depending on the size of the pond or reservoir. For small ponds, shovels and pickaxes may suffice, while larger ponds may require the use of a backhoe or excavator. It is important to ensure that the sides of the pond or reservoir are sloped gradually to prevent erosion.

4. Lining
To prevent the water from seeping into the ground, the pond or reservoir should be lined with a suitable material. This can be done using clay, bentonite, or a synthetic liner made of rubber or plastic. The lining should be placed carefully to ensure that it covers the entire bottom and sides of the pond or reservoir.

5. Filling
Once the lining is in place, the pond or reservoir can be filled with water. It is important to fill the pond or reservoir gradually to allow the lining to settle and prevent any leaks. The pond or reservoir should be filled to a level that is safe for the surrounding area, taking into consideration factors such as soil type and slope.

6. Maintenance
After the pond or reservoir has been filled, it is important to maintain it properly. This includes regular inspections for any leaks, as well as

removing any debris that may accumulate in the pond or reservoir. If the pond or reservoir is used for livestock, it is important to ensure that the water is clean and free from any harmful bacteria.

Digging a pond or reservoir for water storage is a significant undertaking, but it can provide a reliable source of water for those living off-grid. Proper planning and execution can help ensure that the pond or reservoir is safe, effective, and provides a valuable resource for the homestead.

2.9 Building a Water Pump Using Recycled Materials

Access to a reliable source of water is essential for off-grid living, and having a water pump can greatly facilitate the process of getting water from a well, pond, or reservoir to your homestead. Building a water pump using recycled materials is an excellent way to minimize your environmental impact and reduce your reliance on expensive or hard-to-find parts.

The first step in building a water pump is to gather the necessary materials. You will need a few pieces of PVC piping, a bicycle wheel, a rubber strip, a few screws, and some tubing. Most of these materials can be found at a hardware store or salvage yard, and you may even have some of them lying around your homestead.

To begin construction, start by attaching the rubber strip to the bicycle wheel. This will act as the pump's diaphragm, pushing water through the tubing when the wheel is turned. Next, drill a hole in the PVC piping and attach it to the wheel using screws. This will act as the pump's housing.

Once the pump is assembled, you can connect it to your water source using tubing. To operate the pump, simply turn the bicycle wheel by hand, and the diaphragm will push water through the tubing and into your storage tank.

It is important to note that this type of pump is best suited for low-volume applications, such as watering plants or filling a small water tank. If you need to pump water for larger applications, such as supplying your home or livestock, you may need to consider a more powerful and reliable pump.

Overall, building a water pump using recycled materials is a fun and rewarding project that can help you become more self-sufficient on your homestead. By reusing materials that would otherwise go to waste, you can reduce your environmental impact and save money on expensive equipment.

2.10 Sterilizing Water in the Sun

Sterilizing water is an essential part of off-grid living, especially if the water source is not completely clean. One of the easiest and most effective ways to sterilize water is by using the sun's ultraviolet (UV) rays. UV radiation can destroy bacteria, viruses, and other pathogens that can cause waterborne illnesses. Here are the steps to follow to sterilize water using the sun:

1. **Find a clear plastic or glass bottle:** For this method to work, the water needs to be exposed to direct sunlight. Therefore, you need to use a clear container, preferably made of glass or plastic.

2. **Fill the container with water:** Fill the container with water from your well, pond, or any other water source you have. Ensure that the container is clean.

3. **Place the container in direct sunlight:** Put the container in an area where it can be exposed to direct sunlight for at least six hours. The water needs to be exposed to the UV rays for an extended period to ensure that all pathogens are destroyed.

4. **Rotate the container:** If possible, rotate the container occasionally to ensure that all sides of the container are exposed to the sun's rays.

5. **Drink the water:** After six hours of exposure to the sun, the water should be sterilized and safe to drink. However, you should still check the water for any impurities before drinking it.

Note that this method is only effective in areas with sufficient sunlight. If you live in an area with low sunlight, you may need to consider other sterilization methods. Additionally, this method does not remove any physical impurities such as dirt or debris. Therefore, it is recommended that you use a filtration method before using this method for sterilization.

Chapter 3:
Heating/Cooling Projects and Medical First Aid

Chapter 3 focuses on two important aspects of homesteading: heating/cooling and medical first aid. When living off-grid, it is essential to have reliable and sustainable sources of heating and cooling to ensure comfort and safety throughout the year. Additionally, being self-sufficient also means being prepared for any medical emergencies that may arise. This chapter provides a range of DIY projects that can help homesteaders achieve these goals, including building efficient stoves and air conditioning systems, as well as learning basic first aid techniques and creating a well-stocked medical kit.

3.1 Heating Projects

Heating is an essential aspect of homesteading, especially during the colder months of the year. There are several options available for heating projects, including wood stove installation, rocket stoves, and solar heating. Each of these methods has its advantages and disadvantages, and the best option for a homesteader will depend on their specific needs and circumstances. In this section, we will explore these three methods in detail, examining the equipment and materials required for each, as well as the benefits and drawbacks of each option. With this information, homesteaders can make an informed decision about which heating project will best suit their needs.

A. Wood Stove Installation

Installing a wood stove is a great way to heat your home during cold weather. Here are some more detailed steps for the installation process:

1. **Choose the right location:** The first step in installing a wood stove is to choose the right location for it. The stove should be located in an area where it will provide the most heat to your home. It should also be near a chimney or vent where smoke can be safely removed from the home.

2. **Install the chimney:** The next step is to install the chimney or vent. The chimney should be made of insulated stainless steel and should be installed according to local building codes. It should also be installed at the correct height to ensure that smoke is removed from the home properly.

3. **Prepare the area:** Before installing the stove, you need to prepare the area where it will be installed. This may involve removing carpeting or other flooring materials, as well as

ensuring that the area is free of flammable materials.

4. **Install the stove:** Once the area is prepared, you can install the stove. This involves connecting the stove to the chimney or vent and ensuring that all connections are secure. The stove should also be leveled to ensure that it functions properly.

5. **Test the stove:** After the stove is installed, you should test it to ensure that it is working properly. This may involve lighting a fire and checking that smoke is being removed from the home efficiently. You should also test the stove's ability to heat your home and adjust the settings as needed.

6. **Maintain the stove:** Finally, it's important to maintain the stove to ensure that it continues to function properly. This may involve cleaning the chimney regularly, replacing parts as needed, and ensuring that the stove is used safely and responsibly.

By following these steps, you can install a wood stove and enjoy the warmth and comfort it provides during cold weather. However, it's important to note that wood stoves can be dangerous if not used properly, so it's important to take the time to install and maintain them correctly.

B. Rocket Stove

A rocket stove is a highly efficient, low-emission wood-burning stove. It is designed to burn small-diameter wood fuel such as twigs, sticks, and small branches. The rocket stove has a unique combustion chamber that maximizes the amount of heat generated from the fuel, making it a popular choice for off-grid living, camping, and emergency preparedness.

The basic design of a rocket stove consists of a combustion chamber, a chimney, and an insulated burn chamber. The fuel is loaded into the combustion chamber, which is shaped like a rocket, hence the name rocket stove. The insulation around the combustion chamber helps to retain the heat, while the chimney draws the smoke and gasses out of the stove.

Rocket stoves are known for their efficient use of fuel. The combustion chamber is designed to promote complete combustion, resulting in less smoke and ash production. The high heat generated by the rocket stove can be used for a variety of purposes, including cooking, heating water, and providing warmth to a living space.

One of the key advantages of a rocket stove is that it can be constructed from locally available materials. The stove can be made from clay, bricks, metal, or other materials that are heat resistant. DIY rocket stove designs are widely available online, and many people have successfully built their own rocket stoves.

Another advantage of the rocket stove is its portability. Many models are lightweight and can be easily transported for use in camping or emergency situations. Some rocket stoves are even designed to be collapsible for easy storage and transportation.

When using a rocket stove, it is important to follow basic safety guidelines. The stove can get very hot, and it should be kept away from flammable materials. Care should be taken when loading fuel into the combustion chamber, and the chimney should be kept clear to prevent the buildup of smoke and gasses.

In summary, the rocket stove is an efficient, low-emission wood-burning stove that is ideal for off-grid living, camping, and emergency preparedness. Its efficient use of fuel, portability, and simple design make it a popular choice for those seeking sustainable and practical heating solutions.

C. Solar Heating

Solar heating is a great way to heat your homestead using renewable energy. There are a variety of methods to capture and use solar energy for heating, including passive solar heating, active solar heating, and solar water heating.

Passive solar heating is a method of using the sun's energy to heat a space without the use of mechanical systems. This can be accomplished by designing your home or building to maximize solar exposure and heat retention, such as through the use of large windows, thermal mass materials, and natural ventilation.

Active solar heating, on the other hand, uses mechanical systems such as solar air heaters or solar water heaters to capture and distribute solar heat. Solar air heaters work by drawing cool air into a collector where it is heated by the sun and then distributed back into the living space, while solar water heaters work by circulating water through a collector where it is heated and then stored in a tank for later use.

Solar water heating is a popular method for providing hot water for domestic use, such as for showers and washing dishes. There are two main types of solar water heating systems: passive and active. Passive systems rely on natural convection and gravity to circulate water through the system, while active systems use pumps to circulate the water.

In addition to heating your home and providing hot water, solar energy can also be used for cooling through the use of solar air conditioning systems. These systems work by using solar energy to power a heat pump, which cools the air in your home or building.

Overall, solar heating is a great way to reduce your dependence on fossil fuels and save money on energy costs. However, it is important to keep in mind that the initial installation costs can be high, so it may not be feasible for everyone.

3.2 Cooling Projects

In hot and humid climates, staying cool can be a challenge. Traditional air conditioning units can be expensive to operate and rely on electricity, which may not always be available in off-grid situations. However, there are alternative cooling solutions that can help keep you comfortable while minimizing your energy usage. This subsection will cover two popular cooling projects: passive cooling and evaporative cooling.

A. Passive Cooling

Passive cooling is an energy-efficient and cost-effective way to keep buildings and homes cool during hot summer months. Unlike active cooling systems such as air conditioning, passive cooling does not require any mechanical equipment or electricity. Instead, it relies on natural ventilation, shading, insulation, and thermal mass to regulate indoor temperature.

One of the key principles of passive cooling is to minimize heat gain by preventing the sun's rays from penetrating the building. This can be achieved by using shading devices such as overhangs, awnings, and louvers to block direct sunlight. Trees and shrubs can also be strategically planted to provide natural shade and to create a cool microclimate around the building.

Another important aspect of passive cooling is to promote natural ventilation to allow hot air to escape and cool air to circulate. This can be done by designing the building with ample windows and ventilation openings such as operable skylights and vents. Cross-ventilation can be achieved by placing openings on opposite sides of the building to create a natural breeze.

Insulation is also a critical component of passive cooling as it helps to keep the indoor temperature stable by reducing heat transfer. Insulation materials such as fiberglass, cellulose, and foam can be added to the walls, roof, and floor to prevent heat from entering the building.

Thermal mass, such as concrete, brick, or stone, can also be incorporated into the building design to absorb and store heat during the day and release it at night. This helps to regulate indoor temperature by creating a natural buffer zone that keeps the interior cool and comfortable.

Passive cooling is a simple and effective way to reduce energy consumption, lower utility bills, and minimize carbon footprint. By incorporating passive cooling strategies into building design and construction, it is possible to create comfortable and sustainable living spaces that are both environmentally friendly and economically viable.

B. Evaporative Cooling

Evaporative cooling is a natural process of cooling air by the evaporation of water. It works by circulating air through a medium, such as a wet cloth or sponge, which then evaporates the water, cooling the air in the process. This technique is commonly used in hot and dry climates, where it can be more energy-efficient than traditional air conditioning.

One popular form of evaporative cooling is the use of evaporative coolers, also known as swamp coolers or desert coolers. These coolers consist of a fan that draws warm air into the unit, where it is passed through a wet pad or filter. As the air passes through the pad, the water evaporates, cooling the air which is then circulated back into the room. Evaporative coolers are most effective in dry climates, where humidity levels are low, and the air can absorb more moisture.

Another form of evaporative cooling is the use of misting systems, which work by spraying a fine mist of water into the air, which then evaporates, cooling the surrounding area. These systems can be used for outdoor spaces such as patios, decks, and pool areas, and are also commonly used in commercial settings such as restaurants and outdoor entertainment venues.

One of the main advantages of evaporative cooling is its energy efficiency. Compared to traditional air conditioning systems, which can consume a significant amount of energy, evaporative cooling systems require far less energy to operate. Additionally, evaporative cooling can also help to increase humidity levels in dry climates, which can help to alleviate health issues such as dry skin and respiratory problems.

However, evaporative cooling is not effective in all climates. In humid environments, the air is already saturated with moisture, making it difficult for the water to evaporate, which reduces the effectiveness of evaporative cooling. Additionally, evaporative cooling may not provide enough cooling power in extremely hot environments, where air conditioning may be necessary.

Overall, evaporative cooling is an effective and energy-efficient method of cooling, particularly in hot and dry climates. Its effectiveness and efficiency make it an appealing option for both residential and commercial applications.

3.3 Medical First Aid

In times of crisis or disaster, medical emergencies can occur, and access to medical care may be limited or nonexistent. As such, it is important to be prepared to handle common medical issues and emergencies using basic first aid techniques and supplies. This subsection will cover some essential first aid skills and supplies that can help you provide effective medical care in emergency situations. From assessing the severity of an injury to administering basic treatments and medications, these techniques can help you stay safe and healthy in challenging circumstances.

A. Basic First Aid Skills

Basic first aid skills are essential for emergency situations where medical assistance may not be immediately available. It is important to have a basic understanding of first aid skills in case of an accident or emergency. Below are some basic first aid skills that can be useful in various situations:

1. **CPR:** Cardiopulmonary resuscitation (CPR) is a lifesaving technique that can help a person who has stopped breathing or has no pulse. It

involves chest compressions and rescue breaths to help circulate oxygenated blood to vital organs.

2. **Stop Bleeding:** Knowing how to stop bleeding is essential in emergencies. Applying pressure to the wound with a clean cloth or bandage can help to slow or stop the bleeding. Elevating the wound above the heart level can also help to reduce bleeding.

3. **Treatment for Shock:** Shock is a life-threatening condition that can occur after a severe injury or illness. Symptoms of shock include cold, clammy skin, rapid breathing, and a weak pulse. To treat shock, lay the person down, elevate their feet, and cover them with a blanket to keep them warm.

4. **Burn Treatment:** Burns can be caused by fire, hot liquids, or chemicals. In case of a minor burn, you can run cool water over the affected area to reduce the pain and prevent further damage. For more severe burns, cover the burn with a sterile dressing and seek medical help immediately.

5. **Dealing with Fractures:** Fractures can be caused by accidents or falls. If you suspect that someone has a fracture, immobilize the injured area by using a splint or bandage. Apply ice to the injured area to help reduce swelling.

6. **Choking:** Choking is a life-threatening emergency that can happen when a person's

airway is blocked. If someone is choking, perform the Heimlich maneuver to help dislodge the object.

It is important to note that these are just basic first aid skills and are not a substitute for professional medical treatment. In case of a medical emergency, it is always best to seek professional help as soon as possible.

B. Herbal Medicine

Herbal medicine is a form of traditional medicine that uses plants and plant extracts to treat various illnesses and promote healing. It has been used for thousands of years and has been a major part of many cultures and societies around the world. Herbal medicine can be used in a variety of forms, including teas, tinctures, capsules, and poultices.

Herbs contain many different compounds, including essential oils, flavonoids, and alkaloids, which can have therapeutic effects on the body. Different herbs can be used for different purposes, such as promoting relaxation, reducing inflammation, improving digestion, and boosting the immune system.

Some commonly used herbs in traditional medicine include:

1. **Echinacea:** This herb is commonly used to boost the immune system and prevent and treat colds and flu.
2. **Ginger:** Ginger is often used to reduce nausea and vomiting, as well as to alleviate pain and inflammation.
3. **St. John's Wort:** This herb is used to treat mild to moderate depression and anxiety.
4. **Chamomile:** Chamomile is often used to promote relaxation and sleep, as well as to soothe digestive issues.
5. **Turmeric:** Turmeric is used to reduce inflammation and relieve pain, and may also have anticancer properties.

Herbal medicine can be a useful addition to traditional first aid treatments, and can be used to treat a variety of conditions such as burns, cuts, and insect bites. However, it is important to remember that not all herbal remedies are safe, and some can interact with prescription medications or cause side effects.

Before using any herbal remedies, it is important to do thorough research and consult with a qualified herbalist or healthcare professional. It is also important to note that herbal remedies should not be used as a substitute for conventional medical treatments in cases of serious illness or injury.

C.Alternative Medicine

Alternative medicine, also known as complementary or integrative medicine, is a broad term used to describe medical practices that fall outside of conventional or mainstream healthcare. These practices may be used in conjunction with conventional medicine or instead of it.

Alternative medicine encompasses a wide range of therapies and approaches, including but not limited to herbal medicine, acupuncture, chiropractic, massage therapy, naturopathy, and energy medicine. Some alternative therapies, such as chiropractic and acupuncture, have gained mainstream acceptance and are commonly used alongside conventional medicine.

One of the core beliefs behind alternative medicine is that the body has the ability to heal itself, and that the goal of treatment is to support this natural healing process. Alternative therapies often take a holistic approach, treating the entire person rather than just the symptoms of their illness.

Herbal medicine is one of the most commonly used forms of alternative medicine. It involves the use of plant extracts, or parts of plants, to treat a variety of health conditions. Many pharmaceutical drugs are actually derived from plant compounds, and herbal medicine seeks to harness the healing power of these natural compounds in a more holistic way.

Acupuncture is another popular form of alternative medicine, which involves the insertion of fine needles into specific points on the body to stimulate energy flow and promote healing. Chiropractic focuses on the manipulation of the musculoskeletal system to alleviate pain and improve mobility.

Massage therapy involves the manipulation of soft tissues to promote relaxation and relieve tension, while naturopathy is a holistic approach to healthcare that incorporates diet, lifestyle changes, and natural remedies to treat illness and promote wellness.

Energy medicine is a more recent addition to the alternative medicine landscape and involves the use of various therapies to balance the body's energy fields and promote healing. These therapies may include techniques such as Reiki, healing touch, or acupuncture.

Alternative medicine is a controversial topic, with some people embracing these therapies as effective alternatives to conventional medicine, while others view them as unproven and potentially dangerous. It is important for individuals considering alternative medicine to do their research and consult with a qualified practitioner to ensure they are receiving safe and effective treatment.

Chapter 4: Waste Management

Managing waste is an essential part of sustainability and responsible living. As we produce more waste than ever before, it's becoming increasingly important to find ways to dispose of it safely and efficiently. This chapter covers several waste management methods, including waste disposal, recycling, and composting.

Subsections:

1. Waste Disposal Methods
2. Recycling and Reusing Materials
3. Composting Waste for the Garden

Each of these subsections provides detailed information on the different waste management methods and how they can be implemented in a sustainable and efficient manner. By learning how to manage waste effectively, we can reduce our environmental impact and create a cleaner and healthier living environment.

4.1 Waste Disposal Methods

Waste disposal is the process of managing and disposing of waste materials in a safe, efficient, and environmentally responsible way. In a survival situation, waste disposal becomes especially important as it can have significant impacts on human health and hygiene.

There are several waste disposal methods that can be used in a survival situation, depending on the type of waste and the resources available. Some of the most common methods include:

1. Landfills
Landfills are large areas of land that are designated for the disposal of waste materials. The waste is placed in the landfill and covered with soil to prevent the release of harmful gases and odors. While landfills are a common waste disposal method, they can have negative environmental impacts, such as soil and water pollution.

2. Incineration
Incineration is the process of burning waste materials at high temperatures to reduce their volume and convert them into ash and gasses. Incineration can be an effective way to dispose of certain types of waste, such as medical waste, but it can also release harmful pollutants into the air.

3. Burial
Burial involves burying waste materials in the ground, often in a designated pit or trench. This method can be effective for disposing of organic waste, such as food scraps, but it can also create pollution and attract pests.

4. Composting
Composting is the process of breaking down

organic waste materials, such as food scraps and yard waste, into a nutrient-rich soil amendment. Composting is an effective way to manage waste in a sustainable way, as it reduces the amount of waste sent to landfills and creates a valuable product for the garden.

5. Recycling

Recycling involves the process of converting waste materials into new products. In a survival situation, recycling may not be feasible, but it is still important to consider how to reuse and repurpose materials to reduce waste.

When choosing a waste disposal method, it is important to consider the type of waste being produced, the available resources, and the potential environmental impacts. By managing waste effectively, it is possible to reduce the risk of disease and pollution, and promote a healthier environment for everyone.

4.2 Recycling and Reusing Materials

Recycling and reusing materials is an essential aspect of sustainable living, as it reduces waste and conserves resources. By recycling and reusing materials, we can decrease the amount of waste that goes to landfills and reduce the need for new materials to be produced.

One of the simplest ways to recycle and reuse materials is to separate recyclable items from other waste and dispose of them appropriately. This can include items such as paper, plastic, glass, and aluminum cans. Many communities have recycling programs in place that make it easy to dispose of recyclable items, either through curbside pickup or at designated drop-off locations.

Another way to recycle and reuse materials is to repurpose items that would otherwise be discarded. This can include using old clothing to make cleaning rags, turning old pallets into furniture, or using glass jars for storage containers. With a little creativity, many items that might otherwise be thrown away can be repurposed and given a new life.

For materials that cannot be recycled or repurposed, it's important to dispose of them in a way that is as environmentally friendly as possible. This may include burying organic waste in a designated composting area or using a waste-to-energy system that converts trash into energy.

Overall, by recycling and reusing materials, we can help to reduce waste, conserve resources, and minimize our impact on the environment.

4.3 Composting Waste for the Garden

Composting is an effective and easy way to manage organic waste and transform it into nutrient-rich soil that can be used to improve garden soil quality. Composting involves the breakdown of organic materials, such as food scraps, yard waste, and other organic matter, by bacteria and other microorganisms. This process generates heat, which can kill harmful pathogens and weed seeds.

To start composting, you will need a compost bin or pile. Compost bins can be purchased or constructed using materials such as wood, wire mesh, or plastic. The bin should be at least 3 feet wide and 3 feet deep to allow for proper aeration and mixing of the materials.

The materials that can be added to the compost bin include fruit and vegetable scraps, eggshells, coffee grounds, tea bags, yard waste such as leaves and grass clippings, and small amounts of shredded paper or cardboard. Avoid adding meat, dairy, or oily foods as they can attract pests and slow down the composting process.

To ensure a proper balance of carbon and nitrogen, known as the C:N ratio, it is recommended to add a mix of "brown" and "green" materials. Brown materials include dried leaves, straw, and sawdust, while green materials include grass clippings, fruit and vegetable scraps, and fresh yard waste.

It is also important to keep the compost pile moist and aerated to support the microorganisms that break down the organic matter. Turning the compost pile every few weeks will help to incorporate air and mix the materials for faster decomposition. A compost thermometer can be used to monitor the temperature of the compost pile, which should ideally reach between 135°F and 160°F to ensure that harmful pathogens and weed seeds are killed.

Once the compost has broken down into a dark, crumbly material that resembles soil, it can be used to improve the soil quality in the garden. Compost can be added to garden beds as a soil amendment, or used as a mulch to help retain moisture and suppress weeds.

Composting is a sustainable and effective way to manage organic waste and improve garden soil quality. With the right materials and techniques, anyone can start composting and contribute to a healthier environment.

Additional tips and information for composting waste for the garden:

1. **Choose the Right Composting Method:** There are several ways to compost your waste, including traditional composting, vermicomposting (using worms), and bokashi

composting (using a special type of fermented bran). Choose the method that works best for you based on the size of your garden, the amount of waste you generate, and the time and effort you are willing to invest.

2. **Collect Composting Materials:** Collect a mix of green (nitrogen-rich) and brown (carbon-rich) materials for your compost pile. Green materials include fruit and vegetable scraps, grass clippings, and coffee grounds, while brown materials include leaves, wood chips, and shredded paper. Avoid adding meat, dairy, or oily foods, as these can attract pests and slow down the composting process.

3. **Build Your Compost Pile:** Start by layering brown and green materials in a pile or bin. Keep the pile moist, but not too wet, and turn it regularly to aerate the compost and speed up the decomposition process. You can also add a compost starter or accelerator to help break down the materials faster.

4. **Use Your Compost:** Once your compost is ready, it should be dark and crumbly, with a pleasant earthy smell. Use it to amend your soil, add nutrients to your plants, and improve soil structure. You can also use compost as a mulch or top dressing for your garden beds.

5. **Troubleshooting:** If your compost pile is not decomposing properly, there may be several reasons, including a lack of moisture, insufficient aeration, or an incorrect balance of

green and brown materials. If you notice an unpleasant odor, it may be a sign of too much moisture or too many green materials. Adjust your compost pile accordingly to ensure a healthy and productive garden.

In conclusion, waste management is an essential part of sustainable living. There are many methods available for waste disposal, recycling, and reusing materials, as well as composting waste for the garden. By utilizing these methods, we can reduce the amount of waste that ends up in landfills, conserve resources, and even create a valuable resource for our gardens.

It is important to remember that waste management is not just an individual responsibility, but also a community effort. Governments, businesses, and individuals must work together to create a sustainable waste management system that is both environmentally friendly and economically feasible.

As we strive towards a more sustainable future, waste management will continue to be an important aspect of our daily lives. By adopting these methods and making a conscious effort to reduce waste, we can make a positive impact on our environment and create a healthier world for generations to come.

Chapter 5: Producing Your Own Food Off the Grid

In order to live off the grid, it's essential to be able to produce your own food. By growing your own fruits and vegetables, raising livestock for meat, milk, and eggs, foraging for wild food sources, setting up a greenhouse for year-round crops, fishing for food, and even keeping bees for honey production, you can create a sustainable and self-sufficient source of nourishment.

5.1 Vegetable and Fruit Gardening

Growing your own vegetables and fruits is an essential part of off-grid living. Not only does it provide fresh and healthy produce, but it also helps reduce your carbon footprint and increases self-sustainability. Here are some tips for starting your own vegetable and fruit garden:

1. **Choose the Right Location:** The ideal spot for a vegetable garden is a sunny, level area with well-draining soil. It's also important to

choose a spot that is protected from strong winds.

2. **Plan Your Garden**: Decide what you want to grow and how much space you'll need. It's important to consider the mature size of the plants you're growing so they have enough room to thrive.

3. **Prepare the Soil:** Soil preparation is key to a successful garden. Start by removing any grass, rocks, or debris from the area. Then, work in compost, manure, or other organic matter to improve soil structure and fertility.

4. **Choose Your Plants:** Select varieties that are well-suited to your growing conditions and climate. Consider planting a mix of vegetables and fruits that mature at different times to ensure a steady supply throughout the growing season.

5. **Plant Your Garden:** Follow planting instructions on seed packets or plant labels. Be sure to space plants properly and water them thoroughly after planting.

6. **Maintain Your Garden:** Regular maintenance is essential to a healthy garden. This includes watering, fertilizing, weeding, and pest control. Regularly inspect your plants for signs of disease or insect damage, and take action as needed.

7. **Harvest and Enjoy:** When your fruits and vegetables are ready to harvest, pick them promptly to encourage more growth. Use them fresh or preserve them for later use.

By following these tips, you can produce your own fresh and healthy food right at home. Not only is it a rewarding experience, but it can also save you money and reduce your environmental impact.

5.2 Raising Livestock for Meat, Milk, and Eggs

Raising livestock for meat, milk, and eggs can provide a sustainable source of protein and dairy products for off-the-grid living. The type and number of livestock will depend on factors such as available space, climate, and personal preferences. Here are some common types of livestock for homesteading:

1. **Chickens**
Chickens are a popular choice for small-scale homesteads because they are easy to care for and provide a steady supply of eggs. They can also be raised for meat. It's important to provide them with a safe and comfortable coop and run area, as well as access to fresh water and feed.
2. **Goats**
Goats are another popular option for homesteaders. They provide milk, meat, and fiber (if you choose a fiber breed). They are also excellent at clearing brush and weeds.

Goats require a sturdy shelter and access to pasture or hay, as well as fresh water and a balanced diet.

3. Cows

Cows are a larger investment, but can provide a significant amount of meat and dairy products. They require a lot of space, as well as access to fresh water and a balanced diet. It's important to have a good understanding of their nutritional needs and to provide regular veterinary care.

4. Pigs

Pigs can be raised for meat and also provide fertilizer for gardens. They require a sturdy shelter and access to pasture or a balanced diet. It's important to properly manage their waste to prevent environmental damage.

When raising livestock, it's important to be knowledgeable about their specific needs and to provide proper care and nutrition. It's also important to have a plan for processing and storing meat and dairy products. With proper planning and care, raising livestock can be a rewarding and sustainable way to produce food off the grid.

5.3 Foraging for Wild Food Sources

Foraging for wild food sources can be a great way to supplement your diet and add variety to your meals, especially if you live off the grid. However, it's important to do it safely and responsibly. Here are some tips for successful and ethical foraging:

1. Know what you're looking for: Before you head out, research what types of plants and fruits grow in your area and what times of year they're available. Learn to identify the plants correctly and understand which parts are edible and which are not.

2. Forage in safe and legal areas: Make sure you have permission to forage on any land, and be aware of potential hazards such as polluted water sources or areas with poisonous plants.

3. Harvest sustainably: Only take what you need and leave enough for the plant to continue to thrive. Avoid over-harvesting and damaging the ecosystem.

4. Respect the environment: Be aware of the impact you're having on the environment as you forage. Don't trample on other plants, and don't leave any trash behind.

5. Prepare and cook properly: Some wild foods may require special preparation to remove toxins or make them safe to eat. Learn the proper methods for cooking and storing wild foods.

Some examples of wild foods that can be foraged include berries, nuts, mushrooms, wild greens, and edible flowers. With some knowledge and practice, foraging can be a fun and rewarding way to connect with nature and add variety to your diet.

5.4 Setting up a Greenhouse for Year-Round Crops

Setting up a greenhouse can be an effective way to grow crops year-round and extend your growing season, even in colder climates. A greenhouse allows you to control temperature, humidity, and light, creating an optimal environment for plant growth.

Here are some steps to setting up a greenhouse for year-round crops:

1. Choose the right location: The location of your greenhouse is crucial. You want a spot that gets plenty of sunlight throughout the day and is protected from strong winds. Also, consider how easy it will be to access the greenhouse for watering and maintenance.
2. Decide on the type of greenhouse: There are different types of greenhouses, such as lean-to, freestanding, and attached. Each type has its pros and cons, so consider your budget, available space, and desired crops when deciding which type to go for.
3. Prepare the soil: The soil in your greenhouse should be rich in nutrients and well-draining. You can use a combination of compost, peat moss, and sand to create a suitable growing medium.

4. Install a ventilation system: Proper ventilation is crucial in a greenhouse to prevent overheating and to regulate humidity levels. You can install vents, fans, or even an automated system that opens and closes vents and windows as needed.
5. Choose the right crops: Some crops are better suited for greenhouse growing than others. For example, tomatoes, cucumbers, peppers, and herbs are popular greenhouse crops. Be sure to choose plants that thrive in warm, humid environments and adjust your planting schedule to match the seasons.
6. Monitor and maintain the greenhouse: Regular monitoring and maintenance are important to keep your greenhouse functioning properly. This includes watering, fertilizing, pruning, pest control, and cleaning.

With careful planning and attention to detail, you can set up a successful greenhouse for year-round crops and enjoy fresh produce throughout the year.

5.5 Fishing for Food

Fishing is a great way to produce your own food off the grid. It can be done in rivers, lakes, and even the ocean. Not only is it a sustainable way to harvest protein, but it can also be a fun and rewarding hobby. However, it's important to have the right equipment and knowledge to ensure a successful catch.

To get started with fishing, you'll need a fishing rod, reel, line, and bait. There are many different types of fishing rods and reels available, so it's important to choose one that fits your needs and experience level. For beginners, a simple spinning rod and reel is a good option. The line should be strong enough to handle the weight of the fish you're trying to catch, but not too thick that it's easily visible to the fish.

Bait is also an important factor in fishing. Live bait such as worms, minnows, or crickets are effective for many species of fish. Artificial lures such as jigs or spinners can also be used to attract fish. It's important to research the type of fish you're trying to catch to determine the best bait and technique to use.

Fishing can be done from a boat or from shore. If fishing from shore, it's important to find a location with easy access to the water and where fish are likely to be found. This could be near rocks, logs, or other underwater structures where fish like to hide. Fishing from a boat allows you to cover more area and access deeper water where larger fish may be found.

It's important to follow fishing regulations and guidelines to ensure the sustainability of fish populations. This may include catch limits, size limits, and fishing seasons. It's also important to properly handle and release fish that are not being kept for consumption.

Overall, fishing is a great way to produce your own food off the grid. With the right equipment and knowledge, you can enjoy a sustainable and rewarding source of protein.

5.6 Keeping Bees for Honey Production

Keeping bees for honey production is a valuable skill for off-grid living. Bees are not only important for pollinating plants but also provide a source of honey, beeswax, and propolis. Beekeeping can also be a lucrative business if done properly.

Before starting a beekeeping operation, it is important to research local regulations and obtain any necessary permits. Beekeeping equipment such as hives, beekeeping suits, and tools should be purchased or built before acquiring bees. The most common type of bee for beekeeping is the honey bee, which comes in different breeds such as Italian, Carniolan, and Russian.

To begin a beekeeping operation, it is recommended to start with two hives. The hives should be placed in a sunny location with good air circulation and a source of water nearby. Bees need access to flowering plants for food, so the location should also have plenty of vegetation.

Beekeeping involves regular hive inspections to ensure that the bees are healthy and producing honey. It is important to use proper protective gear when inspecting hives, as bees can become agitated and sting. Honey can be harvested once the honeycomb is filled with honey and the bees have capped it with wax. Honeycomb can be removed from the hive and the honey can be extracted using a honey extractor or by crushing and straining the honeycomb.

Aside from honey, beeswax and propolis can also be harvested from the hive. Beeswax can be used for candles, cosmetics, and other products. Propolis, a sticky substance that bees use to seal the hive and protect against infections, can be used in natural medicine.

In conclusion, keeping bees for honey production is a valuable skill for off-grid living. With proper research and equipment, beekeeping can provide a sustainable source of honey, beeswax, and propolis.

5.7 Building an Aquaponics System

Aquaponics is a sustainable and efficient method of growing crops and fish in a closed-loop system. It combines aquaculture, the raising of fish, with hydroponics, the growing of plants without soil, to create a symbiotic ecosystem where both the fish and the plants thrive. Building an aquaponics system can be a great way to produce your own food off the grid and provide fresh fish and vegetables for your family.

There are several components to an aquaponics system, including a fish tank, a grow bed, a pump, and a filtration system. The fish tank is where the fish are raised and their waste products are collected. The grow bed is where the plants are grown, and it is filled with a growing medium such as gravel or expanded clay pellets. The pump circulates water from the fish tank to the grow bed, and the filtration system removes any excess waste products from the water before it is returned to the fish tank.

To build an aquaponics system, you will need to start with a suitable location that receives enough sunlight for your plants to grow. You will also need to decide on the size of your system based on the amount of space you have available and the amount of food you want to produce. Once you have a location and a size in mind, you can start gathering materials.

The first step in building an aquaponics system is to construct the fish tank. This can be made from a variety of materials such as plastic, fiberglass, or even repurposed materials such as an old bathtub or water trough. The size of your fish tank will depend on the number and size of fish you plan to raise.

Next, you will need to construct the grow bed. This can be made from wood, plastic, or other materials, and it should be elevated above the fish tank to allow the water to flow freely between the two. The grow bed should also be filled with a growing medium such as gravel or expanded clay pellets, which will provide support for the plants and allow the water to flow through easily.

Once you have constructed the fish tank and grow bed, you can connect them with a pump and tubing to circulate the water. You will also need to add a filtration system to remove any excess waste products from the water and keep it clean for the fish and plants.

Finally, you can add fish and plants to your aquaponics system. It is important to choose fish and plants that are well-suited to the environment you have created and that can thrive in the same water conditions. Some popular fish for aquaponics systems include tilapia, catfish, and trout, while common plants include lettuce, herbs, and tomatoes.

Building an aquaponics system can be a rewarding and sustainable way to produce your own food off the grid. With careful planning and attention to detail, you can create a thriving ecosystem that provides fresh fish and vegetables for your family year-round.

Chapter 6: Preserving Food for Off-Grid Survival

When you're living off the grid, one of the most important skills to learn is how to preserve your own food. With no electricity or refrigeration, it's crucial to have a plan in place for keeping your food fresh and safe to eat. In this chapter, we'll explore a variety of food preservation techniques that are well-suited to off-grid living.

6.1 Canning

Canning is a popular food preservation method that involves the use of heat to kill bacteria and other microorganisms in food, and then sealing it in airtight jars. This prevents spoilage and allows the food to be stored for long periods of time without refrigeration.

The canning process involves several steps. First, the food is prepared by washing and cutting it into appropriate sizes. Then, the food is packed into clean glass jars, leaving some space at the top. A lid is placed on the jar, and a ring is tightened to hold the lid in place.

The jars are then placed in a pressure canner or boiling water bath canner, depending on the type of food being canned. The canner is heated to a specific temperature and held there for a specific amount of time, which varies depending on the food being canned.

After the appropriate processing time has passed, the canner is removed from the heat and allowed to cool. As the jars cool, a vacuum seal is formed, which prevents air and bacteria from entering the jar.

Canning is a versatile preservation method that can be used to preserve a wide variety of foods, including fruits, vegetables, meats, and soups. It allows you to enjoy the taste and nutrition of fresh, home-grown or locally sourced produce all year round.

However, it is important to note that canning can be dangerous if not done properly. Botulism, a rare but serious illness caused by a toxin produced by the Clostridium botulinum bacteria, can occur if canned foods are not processed correctly. It is important to follow proper canning procedures and guidelines to ensure food safety

6.2 Fermenting

Fermenting is a traditional method of preserving food that has been used for thousands of years. Fermentation occurs when microorganisms, such as bacteria and yeast, break down sugars and starches in food, producing lactic acid and other compounds that inhibit the growth of harmful bacteria. This process not only extends the shelf life of food but also enhances its flavor and nutritional value.

Fermenting is a simple process that can be done with a few basic tools and ingredients. The most common types of fermented foods include sauerkraut, kimchi, pickles, kefir, yogurt, and kombucha.

To start fermenting, you will need a fermentation vessel, such as a glass jar, crock, or fermentation kit, as well as the food you want to ferment and a starter culture, such as whey, brine, or a commercial starter. You will also need to create a brine solution by dissolving salt in water and adding it to the fermentation vessel.

The process of fermenting food can take anywhere from a few days to several months, depending on the type of food and the temperature at which it is fermented. During fermentation, you will need to check on your food regularly to ensure that it is not contaminated with harmful bacteria. You may also need to skim off any scum or mold that forms on the surface of the brine.

Once your food has finished fermenting, you can store it in the refrigerator or a cool, dark place for several months. Fermented foods can be eaten as a snack or used in cooking to add flavor and nutrition to meals.

Fermenting is a sustainable way to preserve food, as it does not require electricity or other energy sources. It is also a way to reduce food waste by using up excess produce that may otherwise go to waste. Additionally, fermented foods are rich in beneficial bacteria that can help improve gut health and boost the immune system.

6.3 Smoking

Smoking is a traditional method of preserving food that has been used for centuries. It involves exposing food, such as meat or fish, to smoke from burning wood or other materials. The smoke contains natural preservatives, such as phenols and creosote, which help to inhibit the growth of harmful bacteria, while also adding flavor to the food.

To smoke food, you will need a smoker, which can be purchased or made at home using materials such as an old refrigerator or a metal barrel. The smoker should have a firebox where the wood is burned, and a chamber where the food is placed for smoking. The wood used for smoking can vary depending on the flavor you want to achieve. Popular woods include hickory, mesquite, applewood, and cherry wood.

Before smoking the food, it should be prepared by curing or brining to help it absorb the smoke and prevent spoilage. Curing involves rubbing the food with a mixture of salt, sugar, and spices, while brining involves soaking it in a mixture of water, salt, and other flavorings. The food should be left to cure or brine for several hours or overnight, depending on the size of the cut.

Once the food is cured or brined, it can be placed in the smoker and smoked for several hours until it reaches the desired level of smokiness. The temperature in the smoker should be maintained at around 200-250°F (93-121°C) for optimal smoking. It's important to monitor the temperature and smoke level throughout the smoking process to ensure the food is cooked properly and not over-smoked.

After smoking, the food can be eaten immediately or stored for later use. It can be kept in the refrigerator for up to a week or frozen for longer storage. When reheating smoked food, it should be heated thoroughly to kill any bacteria that may have grown during storage.

Smoking is a great way to preserve meat, fish, and other foods off-grid, as it doesn't require electricity or refrigeration. With the right equipment and techniques, you can enjoy delicious smoked foods all year round.

6.4 Dehydrating

Dehydrating is a method of preserving food by removing its moisture content, which inhibits the growth of bacteria, yeast, and mold. This process also concentrates the flavors and nutrients of the food, making it an excellent way to store fruits, vegetables, and meats for long-term use.

To dehydrate food, you will need a dehydrator or an oven with a low temperature setting. You can also use the sun, but this method takes longer and requires more monitoring.

Here are the steps for dehydrating food:

1. Choose fresh, ripe produce or lean meats. Wash fruits and vegetables and remove any stems, seeds, or pits. Cut meats into thin slices.
2. Arrange the food on the dehydrator trays, making sure there is enough space between each piece for proper air circulation. If using an oven, place the food on a baking sheet lined with parchment paper.
3. Set the dehydrator to the appropriate temperature and time for the type of food you are drying. For example, fruits typically dry at 135°F for 8-12 hours, while meats require a higher temperature of 155°F for 4-6 hours.
4. If using an oven, set the temperature to the lowest possible setting (usually around 170°F) and prop open the door slightly to allow for air circulation. Check the food periodically and rotate the trays if necessary.
5. Once the food is dry and crisp, remove it from the dehydrator or oven and let it cool completely. Store it in airtight containers or vacuum-sealed bags.

Dehydrated foods can last for months or even years when stored properly in a cool, dry place. They make great snacks for camping or hiking trips, and can also be rehydrated and used in soups, stews, and other recipes.

6.5 Root Cellaring

Root cellaring is a method of preserving fresh fruits and vegetables for off-grid survival. It involves storing produce in a cool, dark, and humid environment to slow down the natural process of decay. Root cellars have been used for centuries and can be a simple and effective way to extend the life of your harvest.

The first step in root cellaring is to select the right location for your cellar. Ideally, it should be in a cool and shaded area with good ventilation. The temperature inside the cellar should be between 32-40°F (0-4°C) with a humidity level of 90-95%.

Next, you will need to construct the cellar. This can be done using a variety of materials, such as cinder blocks, wood, or even old tires. The walls should be insulated with straw, sawdust, or another insulating material. The floor should be made of dirt or gravel to help maintain the desired humidity level.

Once your cellar is complete, you can begin storing your produce. Vegetables like potatoes, carrots, beets, and turnips should be stored in a layer of sand or sawdust to keep them from drying out. Apples and pears can be stored in baskets or boxes, while root crops like onions and garlic can be hung in mesh bags.

It is important to regularly check your stored produce for spoilage and remove any that have gone bad. You should also monitor the temperature and humidity levels in the cellar and make adjustments as needed to ensure optimal conditions.

In addition to providing a means of preserving fresh produce, root cellars can also be used to store other items, such as canned goods, grains, and even wine. With a little effort and planning, a root cellar can be a valuable asset for anyone looking to live off the grid and be self-sufficient.

6.6 Pickling

Pickling is a food preservation method that has been used for centuries. It involves preserving vegetables or fruits in a brine solution made of vinegar, salt, sugar, and spices. The acidity of the vinegar helps prevent the growth of harmful bacteria, while the salt and sugar help to draw out the moisture from the vegetables or fruits, which further inhibits bacterial growth.

To pickle vegetables, start by selecting fresh produce that is free from blemishes, bruises, or soft spots. Wash and trim the vegetables and cut them into desired sizes and shapes. Then, prepare the pickling brine by combining vinegar, salt, sugar, and spices in a large pot and bring it to a boil.

Once the brine is ready, you can either pack the vegetables into jars and pour the hot brine over them, or you can heat the jars and brine together and then pack the hot vegetables into the jars. It is important to follow proper canning procedures to ensure the safety and shelf life of the pickled vegetables.

Some popular pickled vegetables include cucumbers, beets, carrots, green beans, and onions. Pickling is also a great way to preserve seasonal fruits like peaches, pears, and watermelon rinds.

Pickled vegetables can be enjoyed as a side dish, snack, or condiment. They can also be used in salads, sandwiches, or as a topping for tacos and burgers. Pickling is a simple and versatile food preservation method that can add flavor and variety to your off-grid diet.

Conclusion

In addition to these techniques, there are many other ways to preserve your food off-grid, including salting, oil-packing, and using natural preservatives like honey and vinegar. By learning a variety of preservation techniques, you can ensure that your food stays fresh and safe to eat, no matter where you are or what resources you have at your disposal.

Chapter 7: Defense Systems in Your Home

Living off-grid means being self-sufficient, but it also means being self-reliant for your own protection. When it comes to protecting your home and loved ones, there are a few defense systems you can put in place to increase your security.

7.1 Reinforcing Doors and Windows

When it comes to home defense, reinforcing doors and windows is one of the most important steps you can take. Burglars and intruders often target homes that have weak entry points, so taking steps to secure them can go a long way in preventing break-ins.

One of the first things you can do is to make sure your doors and windows are made from sturdy materials. Solid wood or metal doors are more difficult to break down than hollow doors. Similarly, windows made from tempered or laminated glass are harder to shatter than regular glass.

In addition to the materials, consider adding reinforcement bars or grates to your windows. These can be installed on the inside or outside of the window and can make it much harder for someone to break in.

Another important step is to install a deadbolt on all of your exterior doors. A deadbolt provides an extra layer of security and can make it much more difficult for someone to force their way into your home.

Finally, consider adding a security system with door and window sensors. These sensors will sound an alarm if someone tries to break in, and can alert you and the authorities if necessary.

By taking these steps to reinforce your doors and windows, you can greatly increase the security of your home and make it much more difficult for intruders to gain entry.

7.2 Installing a Security System

Installing a security system is an important step towards ensuring the safety and security of your off-grid home. There are many different types of security systems available on the market, each with their own set of features and capabilities. Here are some key factors to consider when choosing and installing a security system:

1. Budget: Security systems can range from simple, low-cost options to more complex and expensive systems. Determine your budget and the level of security you need before selecting a system.
2. Types of sensors: Different sensors can detect different types of threats. Common types of sensors include motion sensors, door and

window sensors, glass break sensors, and smoke detectors. Choose sensors based on the specific threats you want to protect against.

3. Monitoring options: Some security systems come with professional monitoring services, where a monitoring center is alerted when an alarm is triggered. Other systems are self-monitored, where alerts are sent directly to your smartphone or email. Decide which monitoring option works best for your needs.

4. Remote access: Many security systems offer remote access capabilities, allowing you to monitor and control the system from your smartphone or computer.

5. Installation: Some security systems require professional installation, while others can be easily installed by homeowners. Consider your level of expertise and choose a system that you can install and maintain yourself.

It's important to remember that no security system is foolproof, and there are always risks involved in living off-grid. However, installing a security system can provide an extra layer of protection and peace of mind.

7.3 Building a Panic Room

Building a panic room in your home can provide a secure and safe place for you and your family in case of an emergency. Here are some important steps to consider when building a panic room:

1. Choose a location: The location of the panic room is crucial. It should be easily accessible and have only one entry point. Preferably, it should be located in the basement or a secluded part of the house that is not easily visible from the outside.

2. Reinforce the walls: The walls of the panic room should be reinforced with solid materials such as concrete, steel, or bulletproof panels. The walls should also be at least 8 inches thick to withstand forced entry.

3. Install a reinforced door: The door of the panic room should be made of steel or solid wood with a steel core. The door frame should also be reinforced to prevent forced entry.

4. Install a communication system: A communication system is essential in a panic room. A two-way radio or a phone line should be installed for emergency communication.

5. Install ventilation and lighting: Proper ventilation and lighting are important for comfort and safety. The panic room should have a source of fresh air and proper lighting for extended stays.

6. Stock the panic room with supplies: The panic room should be stocked with essential supplies such as water, food, medical supplies, and a first aid kit. It is also important to have a means of sanitation, such as a portable toilet.

7. Plan an escape route: In case of a long-term emergency, it is important to have a plan to leave the panic room. A hidden escape route or a tunnel leading to a safe location can be a good option.

Building a panic room can be expensive, but it can provide peace of mind in case of an emergency. With proper planning and preparation, a panic room can be a safe haven for you and your family.

7.4 Self-Defense Training

In addition to physical barriers and security systems, self-defense training can be an effective way to defend yourself and your home in case of an intruder. Self-defense training can provide you with the skills and confidence necessary to protect yourself and your family, and can also help you to be more aware of potential threats and how to avoid them.

There are many different types of self-defense training available, including martial arts, boxing, and Krav Maga. The type of training that is best for you will depend on your personal preferences and physical abilities, as well as the specific threats you are concerned about.

Martial arts training can help you develop balance, strength, and agility, as well as teach you specific techniques for defending yourself against an attacker. Boxing training can improve your reflexes and help you develop powerful punches, while Krav Maga focuses on real-world self-defense scenarios and is designed to be easy to learn and use under stress.

It's important to remember that self-defense training is not just about physical techniques. Many self-defense courses also cover topics such as situational awareness, conflict resolution, and how to de-escalate a potentially violent situation. By learning these skills, you may be able to avoid physical confrontations altogether.

In addition to taking a self-defense course, it's also important to practice regularly and stay in shape. Self-defense techniques require muscle memory and repetition, so it's important to continue practicing even after you have completed a course.

Overall, self-defense training can be a valuable tool for protecting yourself and your home. By developing the skills and confidence necessary to defend yourself, you can improve your chances of staying safe in a dangerous situation.

7.5 Firearm Ownership

Firearm ownership can be a contentious issue, but for those living off the grid and in remote areas, it can be a necessary part of their defense system. Here are some things to consider when it comes to firearm ownership:

1. Research local laws: It's important to research and understand the local, state, and federal laws when it comes to firearm ownership. Some areas may have restrictions

on certain types of firearms or require special licenses or permits.

2. Safety training: Proper safety training is essential for anyone handling firearms. There are many courses available that teach gun safety and handling techniques. It's important to get training before purchasing a firearm.

3. Choose the right firearm: There are many different types of firearms available, including handguns, shotguns, and rifles. The right type of firearm will depend on your needs and preferences. For example, if you are primarily concerned with self-defense, a handgun may be a better choice than a rifle.

4. Storage: Proper storage of firearms is critical for safety. Firearms should be kept in a locked safe or cabinet, and ammunition should be stored separately.

5. Regular maintenance: Firearms require regular maintenance to ensure they are functioning properly. This includes cleaning and lubricating the firearm, as well as checking for any damage or wear and tear.

6. Responsible use: It's important to use firearms responsibly and only for their intended purpose, whether that be self-defense or hunting. Careless or irresponsible use of firearms can result in injury or death.

7. Consider alternatives: Firearms are not the only option for self-defense. Other alternatives, such as pepper spray or tasers, may be a better choice for some individuals.

Overall, firearm ownership is a serious responsibility that should not be taken lightly.

It's important to consider all of the factors involved before making the decision to own a firearm.

Conclusion

Having defense systems in place can provide peace of mind and increase your security while living off-grid. Reinforcing doors and windows, installing a security system, building a panic room, learning self-defense techniques, and owning a firearm are all ways to enhance your home's security. Remember to always prioritize safety and seek proper training and advice before implementing any defense system.

Chapter 8: Making Money from Your Homestead

Living off-grid can require a lot of self-sufficiency, but it doesn't have to be a completely self-contained lifestyle. Homesteaders can still participate in the economy by generating income from their land and skills. Here are some ways to make money from your homestead.

8.1 Selling Your Homestead Products

Selling your homestead products is a great way to make money and become more self-sufficient. Whether you grow fruits and vegetables, raise livestock, or make your own crafts and products, there is always a market for these goods.

One of the best ways to sell your homestead products is by attending farmers markets or setting up a farm stand on your property. This allows you to interact with potential customers and build relationships with local consumers. It also provides the opportunity to sell a variety of products, from fresh produce to handmade soaps and candles.

Another way to sell your homestead products is through online marketplaces such as Etsy or Amazon. These platforms allow you to reach a wider audience and sell your products to customers all over the world. Online marketplaces are especially useful for selling crafts and specialty products that may not be as readily available in local stores.

You can also consider partnering with local restaurants, grocery stores, and other businesses to sell your homestead products. Many chefs and retailers are looking for fresh, locally sourced ingredients and products to use in their menus and store shelves.

It is important to price your products appropriately to cover the cost of materials and labor, while also making a profit. Researching local market prices and setting fair prices for your products will help ensure that you are able to sell your goods and make a profit.

Selling your homestead products can be a great way to generate income and become more self-sufficient. By using a combination of different sales channels and pricing your products appropriately, you can create a successful business selling the products that you grow and make on your homestead.

8.2 Selling Crafts and Handmade Goods

One potential way to make money from your homestead is by selling crafts and handmade goods. If you have a talent for creating handmade items such as candles, soap, jewelry, pottery, or woodworking, you can turn that talent into a profitable business.

To start selling your crafts and handmade goods, you can start by setting up an online store on websites such as Etsy or Amazon Handmade. These platforms allow you to easily create a storefront, list your products, and handle transactions. You can also create a website or social media presence to promote and sell your products.

Another way to sell your handmade items is by attending craft fairs and farmers markets. These events provide a great opportunity to showcase your products and meet potential customers. Make sure to have plenty of inventory on hand and display your items in an attractive and eye-catching way.

When selling your crafts and handmade goods, it's important to price your items appropriately. Consider the cost of materials, the time it takes to create each item, and any additional expenses such as packaging and shipping. Don't undervalue your work, but also make sure your prices are competitive.

To increase your sales and grow your business, consider offering custom orders or creating themed gift sets. You can also offer discounts or promotions during holiday seasons or other special events.

By selling your crafts and handmade goods, you can turn your homestead into a profitable venture while also showcasing your creativity and skills. With dedication and hard work, you can build a successful business and enjoy the satisfaction of providing high-quality, unique products to your customers.

8.3   Offering   Homestead Services

In addition to selling products and crafts, you can also offer homestead-related services to make money from your off-grid lifestyle. There are many potential services that you can offer, depending on your skills and interests.

One option is to offer homesteading workshops or classes. You could teach people how to garden, raise chickens, or make their own soap, for example. If you have experience with renewable energy, you could also offer classes on solar panel installation or wind turbine construction.

Another service you could offer is farm-to-table meals or catering. If you grow your own vegetables and raise livestock, you could prepare and sell meals made from your own produce. Alternatively, you could cater events like weddings and parties with your farm-fresh ingredients.

If you have construction skills, you could also offer building or renovation services for other off-gridders. This could include building tiny homes, barns, or other structures, or installing off-grid infrastructure like solar panels or rainwater collection systems.

Finally, if you have a talent for writing or photography, you could also offer freelance services to homesteading publications or blogs. Many homesteading magazines and websites are looking for content related to off-grid living, and they may be willing to pay for well-written articles or high-quality photographs.

The key to offering successful homestead services is to identify what you're good at and what people in your community are looking for. By providing high-quality, valuable services, you can generate income while also sharing your love of off-grid living with others.

8.4 Renting Out Your Homestead Property

Renting out your homestead property can be an excellent way to generate income and offset the costs of maintaining your land. Here are some things to consider when renting out your homestead property:

1. Determine what type of rental property you want to offer: You can rent out a portion of your homestead for camping, RVing, or cabin rentals. You can also rent out your entire homestead property as a vacation rental, long-term rental, or short-term rental.

2. Research local zoning and rental laws: Check with your local government to ensure that your property is zoned for rentals and that you have all necessary permits and licenses. Additionally, research local rental laws and regulations to ensure that you are in compliance with all requirements.

3. Prepare your property for rental: Ensure that your property is clean and well-maintained. If you are renting out a portion of your property for camping or RVing, ensure that you have the necessary amenities such as water and electrical hookups, fire pits, and picnic areas. If you are renting out a cabin or vacation rental, ensure that it is fully furnished and equipped with everything your guests may need.

4. Set competitive rental rates: Research similar properties in your area to determine what rental rates are competitive. Consider offering discounts for longer stays or offseason rentals.

5. Market your property: List your property on rental websites and social media platforms. Highlight the unique features of your homestead property, such as access to hiking trails, nearby fishing or hunting areas, or the opportunity to interact with farm animals.

6. Screen potential renters: Once you have inquiries from potential renters, conduct a

background check and credit check to ensure that they are reliable and responsible tenants.

7. Create a rental agreement: Develop a rental agreement that outlines the terms and conditions of the rental, including payment schedules, security deposits, and house rules.

8. Maintain communication with your renters: Ensure that you maintain regular communication with your renters to address any concerns or issues that may arise during their stay.

Renting out your homestead property can be a great way to generate income while sharing the beauty and bounty of your land with others. However, it is essential to ensure that you are in compliance with all local regulations and that you take the necessary steps to prepare and maintain your property for rental.

8.5 Starting a Homestead Business

Starting a homestead business can be an excellent way to generate income while living off the grid. Here are some ideas for homestead businesses you can start:

1. Farm-to-Table Restaurant: If you have a talent for cooking and enjoy growing your own produce, starting a farm-to-table restaurant can be a great way to share your homestead

products with others while making money. You can offer fresh, organic meals made from your own vegetables, fruits, meats, and eggs.

2. Organic Produce Delivery: Many people today are interested in eating healthy, organic produce but don't have the time or ability to grow it themselves. You can offer a service where you deliver fresh produce straight from your homestead to local customers.

3. Farmstand: If you have a busy road near your homestead, setting up a farmstand is a great way to sell your surplus produce and handmade goods. You can offer a variety of products, such as vegetables, fruits, eggs, honey, crafts, and homemade baked goods.

4. Bed and Breakfast: If you have a spare room or guest house on your property, you can turn it into a bed and breakfast for tourists. People who are interested in experiencing the homesteading lifestyle will love staying on your property and enjoying your homestead products.

5. Homestead Tour Guide: If you're passionate about homesteading and have experience in farming and gardening, you can offer guided tours of your property to visitors. You can educate them on how to grow their own produce, raise livestock, and live off the grid.

6. Homemade Soap and Skincare Products: If you have experience in soap and skincare product making, you can start selling your homemade products online or at local markets. You can use natural ingredients grown on your homestead to create unique and organic products.

7. Farm Animal Boarding: If you have experience in raising farm animals, you can offer boarding services to other homesteaders who need a place to board their animals while they're away. You can provide a safe and caring environment for the animals and generate income in the process.

Making money from your homestead can be an excellent way to achieve financial independence while living off the grid. There are various ways to make money from your homestead, such as selling your homestead products, offering homestead services, renting out your homestead property, starting a homestead business, and selling crafts and handmade goods. Each of these options requires effort and planning, but with the right approach, it can be a rewarding experience that enables you to generate income while living a self-sufficient lifestyle. By creating a viable income stream, you can also increase your resilience and independence, which is essential in the face of unexpected events or emergencies.

Conclusion

Creating and maintaining a homestead off-grid is a complex and rewarding lifestyle that requires a great deal of planning, hard work, and knowledge. This book has provided an overview of the essential aspects of homesteading, including selecting a suitable location, building a shelter, producing food, managing waste, and protecting yourself and your property.

To establish a successful off-grid homestead, it is crucial to have a deep understanding of the land, climate, and natural resources in your area. This knowledge is necessary to make informed decisions about building structures, growing crops, and raising animals. Moreover, a good understanding of basic survival skills such as first aid, self-defense, and waste management is critical to ensure the safety and well-being of yourself and your family.

A key component of off-grid homesteading is producing your own food through gardening, raising livestock, foraging, and fishing. It requires skills such as soil preparation, irrigation, seed selection, animal husbandry, and food preservation techniques like canning, fermenting, smoking, and dehydrating. Through these efforts, homesteaders can ensure a steady supply of nutritious food for their families.

To supplement income, homesteaders can explore various business opportunities, such as selling homestead products, offering services, renting out properties, or starting a homestead business. These ventures not only provide additional income but also help promote sustainable living and self-sufficiency.

Finally, homesteading off-grid is a lifestyle that values simplicity, sustainability, and independence. It requires a willingness to learn, adapt, and work hard to create a harmonious relationship with the environment. Although it is not an easy lifestyle, the rewards of self-sufficiency, autonomy, and connection with nature are priceless.

Overall, this book has provided a comprehensive guide to help readers start and succeed in their homesteading journey off-grid. By following the principles outlined in this book, homesteaders can enjoy a fulfilling and sustainable lifestyle that offers freedom, self-sufficiency, and a deep connection with nature.

Made in the USA
Middletown, DE
13 October 2023

40722529R00076